SEAFOOD

SEAFOOD

simple recipes with delicious results every time

Jessica Adair

NEW
HOLLAND

Contents

INTRODUCTION

When buying fish, make sure it is fresh, and if you plan to freeze it, don't buy fish that has already been frozen. There are a few things to look for to tell if fish is fresh.

- It should not have a strong odour. Instead it should have a pleasant and mild 'sea' smell.
- The flesh should be firm with a smooth, slippery skin and no yellow discolouration.
- Whole fish should have bright eyes and red gills.

If you are worried about children swallowing bones, look for the many cuts available without bones. Try flake (also boneless hake), swordfish, marlin, tuna, blue grenadier, sea perch, salmon, John Dory, tail-pieces of ocean trout, ling and blue-eye cod. You will also find that many fish mongers now sell de-boned fillets such as salmon and trout.

If the fish has been packed in a plastic bag, unwrap it as soon as you get home and place it in a glass or stainless steel dish.

Cover lightly with a damp tea towel and keep in the coolest part of the refrigerator.

Use as soon as possible, and if not using the next day, place over a pan of ice.

If freezing, wrap fillets individually in cling wrap for easy separation. Always defrost in the refrigerator or microwave, or cook from frozen. Never thaw at room temperature, and never refreeze thawed fish.

Preparing fish

The two types of fish discussed here are described as flatfish (for example, flounder or sole) and round fish (for example, snapper or cod). Both types need to be cleaned before use, but cleaning procedures vary.

Scaling and finning

Most fish will need to be scaled. However, there are a few exceptions, such as trout, tuna, shark, leatherjacket and others. When poaching a whole unboned fish, it is best to leave the dorsal and anal fins attached. This will help to hold the fish together during cooking.

Wash fish and leave wet, as a wet fish is easier to scale. Remove scales using a knife or scaler, starting at the tail and scraping towards the head (picture 1).

Clip the dorsal fin with scissors or, if desired, remove both the dorsal and anal fins by cutting along the side of the fin with a sharp knife. Then pull the fin towards the head to remove it (picture 2).

Gutting

Gutting techniques are different for round fish and flatfish. When preparing fish to bone or fillet, remove the entrails by gutting through the belly. If you wish to serve the fish whole, preserve the shape of the fish by gutting through the gills.

Round fish

For boning or filleting, cut off the head behind gill opening. Use a sharp knife and cut open the belly from head to just above anal fin (picture 3). Remove membranes, veins and viscera. Rinse thoroughly.

To preserve shape of round fish, cut through the gills (picture 4) and open outer gill with the thumb. Put a finger into the gill and snag the inner gill. Gently pull to remove inner gill and viscera. Rinse well.

Flatfish

To gut, make a small cut behind gills and pull out viscera (picture 5).

Skinning

The tasty skin of some fish enhances the flavor. However, other fish have strong or inedible skin that interferes with the flavor. Always leave skin on when poaching or grilling a whole fish.

Round fish

When skinning a whole round fish, make a slit across the body behind the gills, with another just above the tail. Then make another cut down the back (picture 6).

Using a sharp knife, start at the tail and separate the skin from the flesh. Pull the knife towards the head, while holding the skin firmly with the other hand – do not use a sawing motion.

Flatfish

To skin a whole flatfish, first turn the dark side up, then cut across the skin where the tail joins the body (picture 7). With a sharp knife, peel the skin back towards the head until you have enough skin to hold with one hand (picture 8).

Anchor the fish with one hand and pull the skin over the head. Turn fish over and hold the head while pulling the skin down to the tail.

Cutting fillets

Fillets are pieces of boneless fish. There are slightly different techniques for filleting round fish and flatfish.

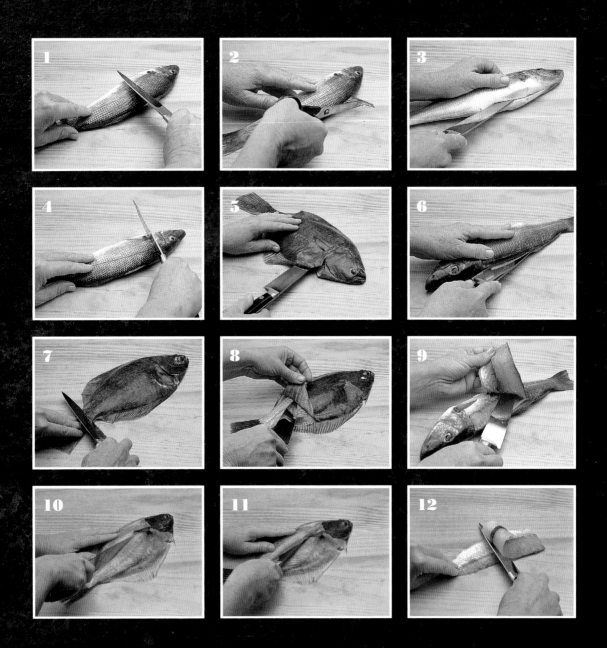

Soft-shelled crabs

Cut across the eyes with a sharp knife. Pull out and discard the stomach sac. Turn over and lift the tail flap or apron and fold it away from the body. Pull out the apron and attached intestinal vein, and discard. Turn crab right-side up and lift flaps on each side near legs. Scrape off and discard spongy gills.

Opening abalone

Using a strong knife, force the blade tip into the thin part of the shell and underneath the flesh. Work blade backwards and forwards until muscle is freed from shell. Lift out flesh, remove intestine and wash flesh well under cold, running water.

Slice off dark heel (sucker pad). Slice the flesh horizontally in two, wrap slices in tea towel and pound well with the side of a meat mallet or cleaver until limp and velvety. Slices can be cut into thin strips or chopped, depending on cooking method.

Cleaning prawns (shrimp)

Most people prefer to remove the head and body shell before eating. However, the entire body of the prawn is edible, depending on the cooking method.

To peel, break off head, place finger on underside between legs, and roll shrimp. The body shell will come away. Then squeeze tail section, and remainder of shell will slip off (picture 22).

Slit down the middle of the outside curve to expose the intestinal vein. Remove it, and wash shrimp under cold, running water (picture 23). It is not necessary to remove the vein from school or smaller prawns. However, veins of larger prawns sometimes contain shell or grit that can affect taste.

Cleaning yabbies

Freshwater crayfish or yabbies can be found in many inland streams. They have very sweet meat in the tail. Usually they are cooked in their shells. To remove the intestinal vein, hold on a firm surface, right-side up (picture 24).

Hold firmly with one hand and pull the tail flap away from the yabby to remove the intestinal vein (picture 25).

Cleaning squid

Squid can be poached, sautéed, fried, stuffed, baked and grilled, but do not overcook as it will become tough.

Rinse in cold water, and then cut off tentacles, just above the eye. Squeeze the thick centre part of the tentacles. This will push out the hard beak, which you should discard (picture 26).

Squeeze the entrails out by running your fingers from the closed to the open end. Pull out the quill and discard (picture 27).

Peel off skin by slipping finger under it. Pull off the edible fins from either side and also skin them (picture 28).

Cleaning lobster

You can purchase whole live or frozen lobster. Also available are uncooked frozen lobster tails and canned or frozen lobster meat.

To kill a live lobster, hold it on its back on a firm surface. With a heavy chef's knife, stab the point into the mouth to severe the spinal cord. You may also stun the lobster by placing it in the freezer for 30 minutes per 500g.

Weigh to calculate cooking time. Place live lobster in a large pot of cold, salty water and bring to simmering point. Simmer, but do not boil, for 8 minutes per 500g.

Hold lobster right-side up on a firm surface. Pierce the shell at the centre of the body behind the head (picture 29).

Cut lobster in half lengthwise, and remove and discard sac near the head and intestinal vein in the tail (picture 30). Remove any 'mustard' from the body and reserve for flavoring your sauces.

Clean the lobster by rinsing under cold, running water.

Cleaning octopus

Cut head from body section, just below the eyes, to remove tentacles. Cut out eyes and clean body cavity. Push beak up through centre of joined tentacles, cut off and dispose.

Wash thoroughly. Pay particular attention to tentacles as the suckers may contain sand.

Skin is difficult to remove from fresh octopus, but it may be left on for cooking. However, to remove skin, parboil in a little water for 5–10 minutes, then skin when cool enough to handle.

To clean small, whole octopus, cut up back of head and remove gut. Push beak up and cut out. Cut out eyes and wash thoroughly.

Starters

Oysters Kilpatrick

MAKES 24

INGREDIENTS

24 oysters, shucked
2 tablespoons Worcestershire
   sauce
175 g (6 oz) rindless bacon
2 cups rock salt
2 tablespoons parsley
lemon wedges, to serve

METHOD

- Preheat grill to medium heat.
- On a baking tray or heatproof plate, place a thick layer of rock salt and arrange the oysters on the tray, on top of the layer of rock salt.
- Top the oysters with bacon and sprinkle with Worcestershire sauce.
- Grill for 8–10 minutes, or until bacon is crisp.
- Garnish with parsley and lemon wedges.

Prawn Cocktail

INGREDIENTS

1 medium Cos (Romaine) lettuce

600 g (1 lb 5 oz) cooked school prawns (shrimp), peeled

2 medium avocados, peeled and sliced

Cocktail Sauce

600 ml (20 fl oz) tomato sauce

15 ml (½ fl oz) fresh lemon juice

60 ml (2 fl oz) thin cream

1 teaspoon Worcestershire sauce

Tabasco red pepper sauce

salt and pepper, to taste

METHOD

- Preheat grill to medium heat.
- On a baking tray or heatproof plate, place a thick layer of rock salt and arrange the oysters on the tray, on top of the layer of rock salt.
- Top the oysters with bacon and sprinkle with Worcestershire sauce.
- Grill for 8–10 minutes, or until bacon is crisp.
- Garnish with parsley and lemon wedges.

Teriyaki, Chili and Ginger Oysters

MAKES 24

INGREDIENTS

80 ml (3 fl oz) mirin

30 ml (1 fl oz) tablespoons
teriyaki sauce

1 medium red chili, seeds
removed and finely chopped

1 cm (⅓ in) piece ginger,
grated

⅓ bunch chives, sliced

24 oysters

METHOD

- Combine mirin, teriyaki, chili, ginger and chives in a small jug. Place oysters in shell on a serving plate, or remove oysters from shell, and place on chinese spoons. Drizzle with dressing and serve.

Garlic Prawns

SERVES 12 AS AN APPETIZER, 8 AS AN ENTRÉE

INGREDIENTS

125 ml (4 fl oz) olive oil
4 large cloves garlic, peeled
15 g (½ oz) coriander
   (cilantro), chopped
½ teaspoon salt
1 kg (2.2 lb) small green
   prawns (shrimp), peeled
   and deveined
chopped chilies (optional)

METHOD

- In a bowl, combine oil, garlic, coriander and salt. Add prawns, cover and let stand for two hours in the refrigerator.
- Preheat oven to 250°C (500°F). Place prawns and marinade in an ovenproof casserole dish and cook for 10 minutes, or until prawns turn pink. Remove garlic cloves.
- Serve as an appetizer on cocktail sticks, or as an entrée in small ramekins.

Fish Pâté

INGREDIENTS

500 g (18 oz) fish fillets,
  skinned
1 spring onion (scallion),
  finely chopped
2 strips lemon peel, finely
  chopped
125 ml (4 fl oz) dry white wine
1 chicken stock cube
60 g (2 oz) butter
salt and cayenne pepper
90 ml (3 fl oz) cream
2 teaspoons lemon juice
1 packet crispbread

METHOD

- Place fish fillets, spring onion, lemon peel, wine and stock cube into a frypan. Simmer gently for 5 minutes or until fish is just tender. Drain fish fillets, reserving liquid. Remove and discard any bones from fillets.
- In a food processor, place boned fish, reserved liquid, butter, salt, cayenne pepper, cream and lemon juice and purée until smooth.
- Spoon into a serving bowl or individual moulds. Refrigerate for several hours.
- Serve with crispbread.

Barbecued Mussels with Teriyaki Sauce

SERVES 2

INGREDIENTS
450 g (1 lb) fresh mussels

Teriyaki Sauce
30 ml (1 fl oz) teriyaki sauce
15 ml (½ fl oz) peanut oil
3 drops sesame oil
2 cm (¾ in) piece ginger,
    finely grated
1 spring onion (scallion),
    finely chopped

METHOD
- Scrub, clean and de-beard the mussels. Using a knife, unhinge and remove the top part of the shell. Scrunch up a long length of foil to help hold the mussels upright as they cook and lay it over a baking tray.
- Place the mussels in an aluminium foil pan. Top each mussel with some of the sauce. Drizzle with oil. Cook for 3 minutes (mussels are cooked when opaque) on a hot barbecue (covered).
- Garnish with spring onion and serve.

Honey Vinaigrette Prawns

SERVES 4

INGREDIENTS

20 prawns (shrimp), heads
   and shells removed, tails
   left on
3 cloves garlic, crushed
30 g (1 oz) wholegrain
   mustard
60 ml (2 fl oz) honey
15 ml (½ fl oz) balsamic
   vinegar
60 ml (2 fl oz) lime juice
125 ml (4 fl oz) light olive oil
30 g (1 oz) butter
2 tablespoons fresh dill,
   chopped
crusty bread, to serve

METHOD

- Heat lightly oiled barbecue plate and cook prawns or grill
  them till heated through. Place garlic, mustard, honey,
  vinegar, lime juice and olive oil in a saucepan.
- Add butter and heat until boiling. Stir through dill and pour
  over prawns. Serve immediately with crusty bread.

Crab Rice Paper Rolls

MAKES ABOUT 22

INGREDIENTS

60 g (2 oz) vermicelli noodles

1 Lebanese (seedless) cucumber, halved lengthwise and seeds removed

4 spring onions (scallions), thinly sliced

½ bunch coriander (cilantro), leaves picked

½ bunch fresh mint, leaves picked

300 g (10½ oz) fresh crab meat

¼ cup lemon juice

30 ml (1 fl oz) sweet-chili sauce

22 small rice paper sheets, about 16 cm (6 in) diameter

Dipping Sauce

60 ml (2 fl oz) sweet-chili sauce

30 ml (1 fl oz) rice vinegar

2 teaspoons fish sauce

METHOD

- Cook noodles in a saucepan of boiling water for 3–4 minutes or until tender. Drain and set aside.
- Cut cucumber in half again lengthwise and thinly slice. Combine noodles, spring onions, cucumber, coriander, mint, crab meat, lemon juice and sweet-chili sauce in a bowl.
- Dip each rice paper sheet in a bowl of very hot water (nearly boiling) until soft. Place four at a time on a clean surface. Place spoonfuls of mixture on the sheets, fold in the edges and roll up. Repeat with remaining mixture and sheets.
- To make the dipping sauce, combine sweet-chili sauce, rice vinegar and fish sauce in a small bowl.

Oysters Mornay

INGREDIENTS

12 large, flat oysters
salt and pepper, to taste
1 tablespoon Parmesan
  cheese, grated

Mornay Sauce

15 g (½ oz) butter
1 tablespoon plain flour
90 ml (3 fl oz) milk
60 g (2 oz) gruyère cheese,
  grated
salt and freshly ground black
  pepper, to taste
1–2 tablespoons fresh cream

METHOD

- Preheat oven to 180°C (350°F)
- Sprinkle oysters with salt and pepper and place under a hot grill for 1 minute. Spread each oyster with mornay sauce to cover. Sprinkle with Parmesan cheese and bake in a hot oven for about 10 minutes or until golden brown. Serve immediately.
- To make mornay sauce, melt butter in a small saucepan. Blend in flour until smooth, then cook for about 2 minutes. Add milk and bring to the boil, stirring continuously.
- Remove saucepan from heat and add cheese. Stir until cheese melts. Season with salt and pepper and add enough cream to make the sauce a good coating consistency.

Spicy Prawn Dip

SERVES 4–6

INGREDIENTS

250 g (9 oz) cream cheese

90 ml (3 fl oz) mayonnaise

125 ml (4 fl oz) seafood cocktail sauce

15 ml (½ fl oz) lemon juice

3 tablespoons spring onions, chopped

1 tablespoon parsley, chopped

125 g (4½ oz) small prawns (shrimp), peeled

1 packet crackers

METHOD

- Combine all ingredients except prawns in a blender or food processor. Blend well.
- Stir the prawns in by hand. Chill until ready to serve. Serve with a selection of crackers.

Salmon Rolls with Horseradish Cheese

MAKES APPROX. 20–25

INGREDIENTS

8 slices of smoked salmon
100 g (3½ oz) soft cheese, or
   cream cheese
1 tablespoon minced
   horseradish
chives, finely chopped
freshly ground black pepper

METHOD

• Combine the cream cheese and horseradish. On a sheet of plastic wrap, slightly overlap the salmon slices. Spread with the cheese and cover with a small amount of ground black pepper. Sprinkle the finely chopped chives on top. Roll up salmon tightly and enclose in the sheet of plastic wrap. Refrigerate. Just before serving cut into slices.

• Note: This can be prepared a few days beforehand and kept in the refrigerator. Cut the roll into slices just before serving.

Alaskan King Crab Roller

MAKES 12

INGREDIENTS

500 g (1 lb 2 oz) cooked
   Alaskan king crab, chopped
1 stalk celery, finely chopped
30 ml (1 fl oz) mayonnaise
2 teaspoons Dijon mustard
15 g (½ oz) capers, chopped
15 ml (½ fl oz) lemon juice
salt and pepper
12 roller buns of your choice
butter
watercress, to serve

METHOD

- In a bowl, combine crab, celery, mayonnaise, mustard, capers, lemon juice, and salt and pepper to taste. Refrigerate until ready to use.
- Slice the rollers part-way, spread with some butter and toast under a grill or in the oven on a medium heat. It won't take long to toast them, so keep an eye on them if you don't want them to burn.
- Fill up the toasted roller buns with the crab mixture and top with watercress.

Oysters in White Wine

SERVES 4

INGREDIENTS

48 freshly shucked small
   Pacific oysters, on the shell
250 ml (8 fl oz) white wine
30 g (1 oz) chives, chopped
1 teaspoon pink peppercorns,
rinsed and roughly crushed
250 g (9 oz) salted butter, in
   2 cm (¾ in) cubes

METHOD

- Check the oysters are grit free – try not to rinse under running water as you lose that lovely saltwater flavor of freshly shucked oysters.
- Boil the wine and simmer for 2 minutes; add the chives and peppercorns and simmer for a minute. Remove from the heat and swirl in the butter to melt and add the peppercorns – combine well.
- Put the oysters, shell-side down, onto the open barbecue grill about 8 at a time – spoon over some of the sauce. When the liquid is bubbling, the oysters are ready to serve.
- Lift from the barbecue and onto either heaped rock salt on a platter to keep the oysters upright or on finely shredded outer lettuce leaves for the purpose. Leave to cool so they can be picked up and slipped out of the shell and into your mouth around the barbecue.

Nut-Crusted Fish Bites

SERVES 4

INGREDIENTS

60 g (2 oz) chopped hazelnuts
60 g (2 oz) fresh breadcrumbs
30 g (1 oz) plain flour
salt and freshly ground black
   pepper
1 large egg, beaten
500 g (1 lb 2 oz) firm-fleshed
   white fish fillets, cut into 20
   even-sized pieces
vegetable oil for shallow
   frying

To serve

lettuce leaves
tartare sauce
vinegar or lemon juice

METHOD

- Mix together the nuts and breadcrumbs in a large shallow bowl. Put the flour into another bowl and season. Put the egg into a third bowl. Dip the fish pieces into the flour, then into the egg and finally into the breadcrumb mixture to coat.
- Heat 1 cm (⅓ in) of oil in a large frypan and fry a third of the fish pieces for 5 minutes or until golden on all sides. Drain on absorbent paper and keep warm while you cook the rest in 2 batches.
- Serve on a bed of lettuce leaves with tartare sauce or sprinkled with vinegar or lemon juice.

- Note: Hazelnuts go particularly well with fish and make a delightful crunchy coating for these tasty bite-sized pieces of tender fish.

Thai Fish Burgers

SERVES 4

INGREDIENTS

500 g (1 lb 2 oz) white fish
  fillets, bones removed,
  roughly chopped
30 ml (1 fl oz) red curry paste
90 g (3 oz) green beans,
  thinly sliced
4 kaffir lime leaves, finely
  shredded
8 Thai basil leaves, finely
  shredded
15 ml (½ fl oz) soybean oil
4 wholegrain rolls, halved
90 g (3 oz) watercress
1 Lebanese (seedless)
  cucumber, very thinly sliced
1 carrot, very thinly sliced

Dressing

15 ml (½ fl oz) sweet chili
  sauce
15 ml (½ fl oz) lime juice
125 ml (4 fl oz) natural
  yoghurt

METHOD

- Place roughly chopped fish in a food processor, add curry paste and process until smooth. Transfer fish paste to a bowl and stir in beans, kaffir lime leaves and basil and mix well to combine. Shape the mixture into four round, slightly flattened patties.
- Heat the oil in a large non-stick frypan, add the patties and cook over a medium heat for 15 minutes, turning once, until they are cooked through.
- Toast rolls and put watercress, cucumber and carrot on each base. Top each roll with a fish patty.
- To make dressing, put sweet chili sauce, lime juice and yoghurt in a bowl and whisk gently to combine.
- Spoon dressing over patties and cover with toasted roll tops.

Prosciutto Prawns with Rocket Aioli

SERVES 4

INGREDIENTS

24 large green king prawns (shrimp), with middle section peeled and deveined

24 bamboo skewers, soaked in water for 30 minutes or metal skewers

12–24 slices prosciutto*

*(this depends on how long each slice is. If really long, cut across to give two equal pieces. Larger prawns will require the whole piece)

Rocket Aioli

4 medium cloves garlic

½ teaspoon sea salt

2 egg yolks

½ teaspoon lemon juice

125 g (4 oz) blanched and well drained rocket

125 ml (4 fl oz) olive oil

METHOD

- Take each prawn and thread it onto a skewer starting from the tail. Roll each prawn in prosciutto so as to cover all the prawn. Store on a plastic wrap-covered plate in the refrigerator until ready to use. The size of the slice of prosciutto will depend on the size of the prawn being used.
- Heat the barbecue to medium-high and oil the grill bars. Place the prawns on the barbecue turning regularly for even cooking. When the tops (head end) of the prawns are completely white, they are ready to eat. The prosciutto wraps around the prawn very tightly as it cooks.
- Serve with the aioli to one side and with lemon and olive oil-dressed rocket leaves.
- For the Rocket Aioli, put the garlic, salt, egg yolks, lemon juice and rocket into the food processor bowl and work for 30 seconds.
- When this mixture is starting to thicken, slowly pour the oil down the feeder shoot. As it takes, you can add the oil a little more quickly until finished. Use immediately or store for up to five days only.

Bacon-Wrapped Prawns

SERVES 24

INGREDIENTS

750 g (1 lb 8 oz) large
  uncooked prawns (shrimp),
  shelled and deveined, with
  tails left intact
8 rashers bacon, rind
  removed

Herb Marinade

¼ bunch fresh oregano,
  chopped
2 cloves garlic, crushed
125 ml (4 fl oz) olive oil
30 ml (1 fl oz) white wine
  vinegar

METHOD

- To make marinade, place oregano, garlic, oil and vinegar in a bowl and whisk to combine. Add prawns and toss to coat. Cover and refrigerate for at least 1 hour or overnight.
- Drain prawns and reserve marinade. Cut each bacon rasher into 3 pieces, wrap a piece of bacon around each prawn and secure with a wooden toothpick or cocktail stick.
- Cook prawns under a preheated medium grill or on the barbecue, turning occasionally and brushing with reserved marinade, for 5 minutes or until bacon is crisp and prawns are cooked.

Smoked Trout Canapés

SERVES 22

INGREDIENTS

200 g (7 oz) smoked trout,
  cut into 28 pieces
30 ml (1 fl oz) extra virgin
  olive oil
15 ml (½ fl oz) lemon juice
½ bunch flat leaf parsley,
  finely chopped
½ red onion, finely chopped
2 teaspoons baby capers,
  drained
salt and freshly ground black
  pepper
pumpernickel cocktail rounds

METHOD

- Place trout on a plate. Combine olive oil, lemon juice, parsley, red onion, capers, salt and pepper in a small jug. Spoon a little dressing over each piece of trout.
- Cover with plastic wrap and place in the fridge until ready to use. Spread pumpernickel rounds evenly with cream cheese. Top with trout and place on a serving plate.

Tempura Oysters

SERVES 4

INGREDIENTS

24 oysters
sunflower oil for deep frying

Dipping Sauce

90 ml (3 fl oz) dark soy sauce
juice of 1 lime

Tempura Batter

75 g (2½ oz) cornflour
75 g (2½ oz) plain flour
small pinch of salt
4 teaspoons toasted sesame
    seeds
180 ml (6 fl oz) ice cold soda
    water
1 lime, cut into wedges, to
    serve

METHOD

- Open all the oysters (see Introduction) and pour off any liquid. Carefully cut the meat out of the deeper shells.
- To make the dipping sauce, combine the soy sauce and lime juice with 90 ml (3 fl oz) water and pour into 4 dipping saucers.
- Heat the sunflower oil to 190°C (375°F).
- Make the batter by sifting the cornflour, flour and salt into a mixing bowl. Stir in the sesame seeds then stir in the ice cold soda water until just mixed. Add a little more water if it seems too thick. The batter should be very thin and almost transparent.
- Dip the oysters one at a time into the batter. Drop into the hot oil and fry for a minute until crisp and golden. Lift out and drain on absorbent paper.
- Return the oysters to their shells and arrange on plates. Serve with lime wedges and the dipping sauce.

Thai Fishcakes with Sweet Chili Sauce and Cucumber Relish

SERVES 4–6

INGREDIENTS

500 g (1 lb 2 oz) white fish fillets,
   finely diced

30 ml (1 fl oz) red curry paste

30 ml (1 fl oz) fish sauce

15 g (½ oz) cornflour (cornstarch)

1 egg, beaten

40 g (1½ oz) finely sliced green
   beans

20 g (¾ oz) finely sliced spring
   onion (scallion)

vegetable oil for deep-frying

125 ml (4 fl oz) sweet chili sauce
   or

125 ml (4 fl oz) spicy cucumber
   relish

Spicy Cucumber Relish

250 ml (8 fl oz) coconut or white
   vinegar

200 g (7 oz) white sugar

splash of fish sauce

1 large continental cucumber

4 small red chilies, finely chopped

40 g (1½ oz) roasted, unsalted
   peanuts, crushed

50 g (1¾ oz) chopped coriander
   (cilantro) including stems finely
   chopped

METHOD

- In a food processor, mince fish to a paste. Add curry paste, fish sauce, cornflour and egg. Combine well.
- Transfer to a bowl and mix in beans and spring onions. Wet hands and shape mix into flat round cakes approximately 5 cm (2 in) in diameter and 1 cm (⅓ in) thick. Deep-fry in vegetable oil until golden brown, about 5–7 minutes. Drain on paper towel.
- Serve with sweet chili sauce and cucumber relish. The secret to fishcakes is not to overwork the fish mixture, otherwise the cakes will be tough and chewy.
- For the Spicy Cucumber Relish, combine the vinegar, sugar and fish sauce in a small saucepan over medium heat. Bring to a gentle boil, stirring occasionally, and cook for 1 minute. Remove from heat and cool to room temperature.
- Peel cucumber, scrape out seeds and dice. Place the cucumber, chilies, peanuts and coriander in a bowl.
- Pour over dressing and toss gently. The dressing can be made one day in advance and refrigerated then added to relish ingredients just before serving.

Salt and Pepper Squid

SERVES 1

INGREDIENTS

1 whole squid
15 g (½ oz) salt and pepper
vegetable oil, for deep-frying
125 g (4 oz) cornflour
  (cornstarch)
4–5 cloves garlic, finely sliced
1 long chili, chopped (remove
  seeds if you want to
  minimise the spiciness)
2 spring onions (scallions),
  green section

METHOD

- Clean the squid, cut the tubes open. Be careful not to cut all the way through.
- Cut the tubes into 4 x 2 cm (¾ in) pieces and place in a mixing bowl with one pinch of the salt and pepper mixture, mix well.
- Heat the oil in a deep fryer to 180°C (350°F).
- Put the cornstarch (cornflour) in a bowl and slowly add in enough water to make a batter with a consistency that is thicker than paint and slightly sticky. Then add in the squid. Use your whole hand to mix the squid with the batter, don't just coat the surface.
- Slowly lower the squid into the hot oil, it should float when ready. Remove from the oil immediately.
- Lightly oil a wok, place over high heat, throw in the garlic for a good stir and then the chili and spring onions. Use as little oil as possible when tossing the spring onions, garlic and chili. You don't want any excess oil to be absorbed into the batter. A good trick is to use a spray vegetable oil, or rub a paper towel with a little oil on it over the wok.
- Finally add the squid, sprinkle with some of the salt and pepper mixture and give it all a good toss. Serve with some of the remaining mixture on the side.

Smoked Salmon Carpaccio with Extra Virgin Olive Oil and Lemon

SERVES 4

INGREDIENTS

60 ml (2 fl oz) extra virgin
  olive oil
50 ml (1½ fl oz) lemon juice
2 teaspoons small whole
  capers
350 g (12 oz) smoked salmon,
  allow 3–4 slices per person
1 small red onion, finely sliced
1 tablespoon parsley, roughly
  chopped
black pepper, freshly ground
extra capers, for garnish

METHOD

- To make dressing, combine the oil, lemon juice and capers in a bowl, and whisk.
- Arrange smoked salmon and onion on serving plates.
- Drizzle the dressing over the smoked salmon, sprinkle with parsley and ground black pepper, and serve. Garnish with extra capers.

Asian-Flavoured Sea Scallops

SERVES 4

INGREDIENTS

20 scallops, in the shell
spray vegetable oil
50 g (1¾ oz) spring onions
   (scallions), finely chopped
15 ml (½ fl oz) thick soy
   sauce
1 teaspoon green ginger,
   finely chopped
1 teaspoon lemongrass, the
   white section only, finely
   chopped
15 ml (½ fl oz) lime juice
1 small green chili, seeds
   removed, finely chopped
7 ml (¼ fl oz) water

METHOD

- Check each scallop to see that it is clean and grit free. Lift each scallop out of the shell and give the shell a film of oil with the spray, then return the scallop. Repeat for all the scallops and refrigerate until ready to cook.
- Mix the remaining ingredients together and spoon a little over each scallop in the shell.
- Lift the scallops and shells onto a medium-hot barbecue grill – only cook a few at a time as they cook quickly. Turn the scallops carefully if you can, otherwise lift the shell from grill and turn the scallop away from the heat. Spoon over a little more sauce, cook for a little longer and serve when they are done to your liking.

Piquant Prawns

SERVES 4

INGREDIENTS

125 ml (4 fl oz) olive oil
6 cloves garlic, minced
50 ml (1½ fl oz) red wine
   vinegar
400 g (14 oz) canned diced
   tomatoes
1 teaspoon red chili flakes
500 g (1 lb 2 oz) large prawns
   (shrimp), shelled and
   deveined
40 g (1½ oz) fresh basil,
   chopped
40 g (1½ oz) fresh coriander
   (cilantro) chopped
salt and freshly ground black
   pepper

METHOD

- Gently warm the olive oil in a large fry pan. Add the garlic and cook for a few minutes. Add the vinegar and tomatoes, continue to cook over a low heat. Stir in the chili flakes. Add the prawns and simmer until just cooked through, turning often, this should take about 5 minutes.
- Remove from the heat. Add the basil, coriander, salt and pepper. Garnish with a few extra coriander sprigs and serve.

Soups
& Salads

Seafood Chowder

SERVES 4

INGREDIENTS

500 g (1 lb 2 oz) fish fillets
   (bream, snapper or cod)
125 g (4 oz) bacon, diced
1 medium onion, chopped
4 medium potatoes, peeled
   and cubed
1 teaspoon salt, or to taste
6 large green prawns (shrimp)
¼ teaspoon freshly ground
   black pepper
350 ml (12 fl oz) evaporated
   milk

METHOD

- Cut fish into bite-size pieces. In a heavy-based frypan, sauté bacon and onion until meat is cooked and onion is golden.
- Drain and put into slow cooker with the fish pieces. Add potatoes, 500 ml (1 pint) of water, salt and pepper.
- Peel prawns and cook for 30 seconds each side or until the shrimp turn bright orange in colour and put aside to add at the end when the chowder has cooked for the required time and then add to warm shortly before serving.
- Cover and cook on low for 5–8 hours. Add evaporated milk during the last hour.

Crab Bisque

SERVES 6

INGREDIENTS

250 g (9 oz) fresh or canned
crabmeat

60 g (2 oz) butter

60 g (2 oz) plain flour

1.25 litre (2½ pints) milk,
scalded

pinch of freshly grated
nutmeg

salt and freshly ground black
pepper, to taste

60 ml (2 fl oz) dry sherry

15 ml (½ fl oz) whipped
cream, to garnish

1 teaspoon paprika, to
garnish

METHOD

- Flake the crabmeat and pass it through a food processor or blender.
- Make a roux by melting butter in a saucepan and blending in flour until smooth.
- Cook for about 3 minutes. Add milk and stir sauce continuously, until thick and smooth. Add nutmeg and season with salt and pepper. Cook gently for 12–15 minutes.
- Add prepared crabmeat and continue cooking for a further five minutes. Just before serving, stir in sherry. Serve hot or cold, top with whipped cream and paprika.

Prawn Bisque

SERVES 6

INGREDIENTS

300 g (10 oz) cooked prawns
(shrimp), shelled and
deveined
½ onion, diced
175 g (6 oz) tomato paste
600 ml (20 fl oz) chicken
stock
125 ml (4 fl oz) thickened
cream
¼ teaspoon paprika
freshly ground black pepper
30 ml (1 fl oz) dry sherry
¼ small bunch chives,
chopped

METHOD

- Place prawns, onion and tomato paste in a food processor or blender and process to make a purée. With machine running, slowly add stock and process to combine.
- Place prawn mixture in a saucepan and cook over a low heat, stirring frequently, for 10 minutes or until the mixture comes to the boil.
- Stir in cream, paprika and black pepper and cook for 2 minutes or until heated through. Stir in sherry, garnish with chives and serve immediately.

Mussel Soup

INGREDIENTS

1 kg (2.2 lb) mussels, cleaned
and scrubbed

1 small onion, sliced, plus ½
onion, finely diced

1 stalk celery, sliced

1 clove garlic, chopped

125 ml (4 fl oz) white wine

1 small carrot, diced finely

50 g (1¾ oz) cauliflower, cut
into florets

½ capsicum (bell pepper),
finely diced

pinch of saffron threads

10 coriander (cilantro) seeds,
cracked

30 ml (1 fl oz) sherry vinegar

60 g (2 oz) butter

30 g (1 oz) plain flour

30 ml (1 fl oz) thickened
cream

salt and freshly ground black
pepper

4 sprigs parsley

¼ small bunch chives,
chopped

METHOD

- Put mussels in a casserole with sliced onion, celery, garlic and white wine. Cook until mussels have opened, stirring frequently to make sure mussels are cooked evenly. Remove mussels and set aside. Strain broth and set aside.

- In a large saucepan on high heat, put 250 ml (8 fl oz) water, the carrot, cauliflower, capsicum, diced onion, saffron and coriander seeds. Bring to the boil and add sherry vinegar. Remove from heat and allow to cool. When cold, strain vegetables from the cooking liquid. Reserve vegetables and cooking liquid.

- In a saucepan on medium heat, melt butter, then add flour, stir with a wooden spoon and cook gently for 2 minutes. Add broth and cooking liquid, whisking with a whisk, and cook until slightly thickened and a smooth consistency.

- Add reserved vegetables, mussels and cream and bring to the boil. Adjust seasoning if necessary and add parsley and chives just before serving.

Chili and Lemongrass Soup

SERVES 4

INGREDIENTS

2 large tomatoes, each cut
  into 6 wedges
3 stalks lemongrass, sliced
  diagonally into 4 cm (1½ in)
  pieces
20 ml (⅔ fl oz) fish sauce, plus
  15 ml (½ fl oz) extra
8 kaffir lime leaves, torn into
  quarters
200 g (7 oz) straw
  mushrooms
12 large raw prawns (shrimp),
  shelled and deveined, tails
  intact
1 red and 1 green bird's eye
  chili, crushed or left whole
juice of 3 limes
1 teaspoon sugar
20 g (¼ cup) mint leaves
20 g (¼ cup) coriander
  (cilantro) leaves
15 ml (½ fl oz) naam phrik
  pao (Thai red chili paste)

METHOD

- Heat 1¼ L (2½ pints) water in a wok or large pot until nearly
  boiling. Add the tomatoes, lemongrass, fish sauce, kaffir lime
  leaves and mushrooms. Bring to the boil and allow to boil for
  2 minutes. Stir and add the prawns. Reduce heat to medium.
- Gently push the prawns under the surface of the broth but
  do not stir at this stage. After about 1 minute, or once the
  prawns are cooked, stir gently.
- Divide the chilies, soup, prawns and vegetables between 4
  large soup bowls. Season each bowl with one quarter of the
  lime juice, sugar, mint, coriander, extra fish sauce and naam
  phrik pao.
- Stir each bowl gently, remove the lemongrass and serve with
  steamed jasmine rice.

- Note: Naam phrik pao is available from Asian food stores.

Prawn and Avocado Salad

SERVES 4

INGREDIENTS

750 g (10 oz) cooked large
    prawns (shrimp)
1 avocado, sliced
1 grapefruit, segmented

Dressing

30 ml (1 fl oz) mayonnaise
30 ml (1 fl oz) sour cream
15 ml (½ fl oz) natural yoghurt
20 g (¾ oz) mint, chopped

METHOD

- Shell and devein prawns. Arrange prawns, avocado and grapefruit on a serving plate.
- To make dressing, combine mayonnaise, sour cream, yoghurt and mint. Drizzle over shrimp and fruit, and serve immediately.

Thai Squid Salad

INGREDIENTS

3 squid tubes, cleaned

200 g (7 oz) green beans, sliced lengthwise

2 tomatoes, cut into wedges

1 small green pawpaw, peeled, deseeded and shredded

4 spring onions (scallions), sliced

1 cup mint leaves

1 cup coriander (cilantro) leaves

1 fresh red chili, chopped

Lime Dressing

2 teaspoons brown sugar

50 ml (1½ fl oz) lime juice

15 ml (½ fl oz) fish sauce

METHOD

- Using a sharp knife, make a single cut down the length of each squid tube and open out. Score parallel lines down the length of squid, taking care not to cut through the flesh. Score in the opposite direction to form a diamond pattern.
- Heat a non-stick chargrill or frypan over a high heat, add squid and cook for 1–2 minutes each side or until tender. Remove from pan and cut into thin strips.
- Place squid, beans, tomatoes, pawpaw, spring onions, mint, coriander and chili in a serving bowl.
- To make dressing, place sugar, lime juice and fish sauce in a screw-top jar and shake well. Drizzle over salad and toss to combine. Cover and stand for 20 minutes before serving.

Chargrilled Baby Octopus Salad

SERVES 4

INGREDIENTS

375 g (13 oz) baby octopus, cleaned

1 teaspoon sesame oil

15 ml (½ fl oz) lime juice

60 ml (2 fl oz) sweet chili sauce

15 ml (½ fl oz) fish sauce

60 g (2 oz) rice noodle vermicelli

125 g (4 oz) mixed salad leaves

250 (8 oz) bean sprouts

1 Lebanese cucumber (seedless), halved

200 g (7 oz) cherry tomatoes, halved

40 g (1½ oz) fresh coriander (cilantro) sprigs, to garnish

2 limes, cut into wedges, to garnish

METHOD

- Rinse the cleaned octopus and pat dry with absorbent paper.
- Put the sesame oil, lime juice, sweet chili sauce and fish sauce in a jug and whisk to combine. Pour over the octopus and coat with the marinade. Cover with plastic wrap and marinate for 4 hours or overnight. Drain and reserve the marinade.
- Put the vermicelli in a bowl, cover with boiling water and allow to stand for 10 minutes or until soft. Drain well.
- Divide the mixed salad leaves among 4 plates, top with the bean sprouts, rice vermicelli, cucumber and tomatoes.
- Cook the octopus on a preheated chargrill or barbecue until tender and well coloured. Put the marinade in a small pot and bring to the boil. Serve the octopus on top of the salad, drizzle with the hot marinade and garnish with coriander and lime wedges.

Seafood Paella Salad

SERVES 4

INGREDIENTS

1 L (2 pints) chicken stock
500 g (1 lb 6 oz) large raw
  prawns (shrimp)
1 raw lobster tail (optional)
500 g (1 lb 2 oz) mussels in
  shells, cleaned
30 ml (2 fl oz) olive oil
1 onion, chopped
2 ham steaks, cut into 1cm
  cubes
500 g (1 lb) rice
½ teaspoon ground turmeric
125 g (4 oz) fresh or frozen
  peas
1 capsicum (bell pepper),
  diced

Garlic Dressing

125 ml (4 fl oz) olive oil
60 ml (2 fl oz) white wine
  vinegar
50 ml (1½ fl oz) mayonnaise
2 cloves garlic, crushed
¼ cup flat leaf parsley,
  chopped
freshly ground black pepper

METHOD

- Place stock in a large saucepan and bring to the boil. Add prawns and cook for 1–2 minutes or until they change colour. Remove and set aside. If using, add lobster tail and cook for 5 minutes or until it changes colour and is cooked. Remove and set aside.
- Add mussels and cook until shells open – discard any that do not open after 5 minutes. Remove and set aside. Strain stock and reserve. Peel and devein prawns, leaving tails intact. Refrigerate seafood until just prior to serving.
- Heat oil in a large saucepan, and onion and cook for 4–5 minutes or until soft. Add ham, rice and turmeric and cook, stirring, for 2 minutes. Add reserved stock and bring to the boil. Reduce heat, cover and simmer for 15 minutes or until liquid is absorbed and rice is cooked and dry.
- Stir in peas and capsicum and set aside to cool. Cover and refrigerate for at least 2 hours.
- To make dressing, place oil, vinegar, mayonnaise, garlic, parsley and black pepper to taste in a food processor or blender and process to combine.
- To serve, place seafood and rice in a large salad bowl, spoon over dressing and toss to combine.

Warm Barbecued Octopus and Potato Salad

SERVES 6

INGREDIENTS

500 g (1 lb 2 oz) baby
  octopus, cleaned
500 g (1 lb 2 oz) pink-skinned
  potatoes
100 g (3½ oz) rocket or mixed
  salad greens
2 Lebanese (seedless)
  cucumbers, chopped
2 green onions, finely sliced

Lime and Chili Marinade

30 ml (1 fl oz) olive oil
juice of 1 lime
1 fresh red chili, diced
1 clove garlic, crushed

Tomato Concasse

4 Roma tomatoes, diced
40 g (1½ oz) fresh coriander
  (cilantro) chopped
½ red onion, diced
90 ml (3 fl oz) balsamic or
  sherry vinegar
15 ml (½ fl oz) olive oil
15 ml (½ fl oz) lemon juice
freshly ground black pepper

METHOD

- To make marinade, place oil, lime juice, chili and garlic in a bowl. Mix to combine.
- Cut octopus in half lengthwise – if very small, leave whole. Add to marinade. Marinate in the refrigerator overnight or at least 2 hours.
- Cook potatoes until tender. Drain and cool slightly, then cut into bite-size chunks.
- To make concasse, place tomatoes, coriander, onion, vinegar, oil, lemon juice and black pepper in a bowl. Mix to combine.
- Line a serving platter with rocket leaves. Top with potatoes, cucumber and onions.
- Preheat a barbecue hotplate or chargrill pan to very hot. Drain octopus and cook on barbecue or in pan, turning frequently, for 3–5 minutes or until tentacles curl – take care not to overcook or octopus will be tough.
- To serve, spoon hot octopus over prepared salad. Top with concasse and accompany with crusty bread.

Seasoned Fish Salad

SERVES 4

INGREDIENTS

60 ml (2 fl oz) sour cream
2 teaspoons cajun or
    moroccan seasoning
4 fillets of fish
60 ml (2 fl oz) olive oil
30 ml (1 fl oz) red wine
    vinegar
15 g (½ oz) brown sugar
¼ teaspoon garlic powder
salt and pepper
1 avocado, sliced
1 capsicum (bell pepper),
    finely sliced
½ red onion, cut into small
    wedges
200 g (7 oz) mixed lettuce
20 g (¾ oz) toasted pine nuts

METHOD

- Combine the sour cream and seasoning and spread over the fish. Line a baking tray with baking paper. Place the fish on the tray and grill for 5 minutes each side or until the fish is cooked through.
- Whisk together the oil, vinegar, sugar, garlic powder and salt and pepper. Place the avocado, capsicum, red onion and lettuce in a bowl. Add the dressing and toss to combine. Divide the salad between serving plates, top with fish and sprinkle with pine nuts.

- Note: You can replace red wine vinegar with any vinegar you have on hand.

Calamari with Lemon and Herb

SERVES 4

INGREDIENTS

90 ml (3 fl oz) lemon juice

3 cloves garlic, crushed

125 ml (4 fl oz) olive oil

1 kg (2.2 lb) calamari, cut into
thin rings

Dressing

90 ml (3 fl oz) lemon juice

90 ml (3 fl oz) olive oil

20 g (¾ oz) flat leaf parsley,
chopped

1 clove garlic, crushed

1 teaspoon Dijon mustard

salt and freshly ground black
pepper

METHOD

- Place lemon juice, garlic and oil in a bowl, add the calamari and marinate for at least 3 hours. If time permits, marinate overnight.
- To make the dressing, place all ingredients in a bowl or jar and whisk well until dressing thickens slightly.
- Heat a little oil in a pan, add the calamari, and cook for a few minutes until cooked through. Alternatively, the calamari can be cooked on a chargrill plate.
- Serve calamari with lemon and herb dressing drizzled over.

Seared Scallop Salad

INGREDIENTS

2 teaspoons sesame oil

2 cloves garlic, crushed

400 g (14 oz) scallops,
   cleaned

4 rashers bacon, chopped

1 cos (romaine) lettuce,
   leaves separated

60 g (2 oz) croutons

40 g (1½ oz) Parmesan
   cheese, shaved

Mustard Dressing

45 ml (1½ fl oz) mayonnaise

15 ml (½ fl oz) olive oil

1 tablespoon vinegar

2 teaspoons Dijon mustard

METHOD

- To make dressing, place mayonnaise, olive oil, vinegar and mustard in a bowl, mix to combine and set aside.
- Heat sesame oil in a frypan over a high heat, add garlic and scallops and cook, stirring, for 1 minute or until scallops just turn opaque. Remove scallop mixture from pan and set aside. Add bacon to pan and cook, stirring, for 4 minutes or until crisp. Remove bacon from pan and drain on absorbent paper.
- Place lettuce leaves in a large salad bowl, add dressing and toss to coat. Add bacon, croutons and Parmesan and toss to combine. Spoon scallop mixture over salad and serve.

Garlic Prawn Salad

SERVES 4

INGREDIENTS

15 ml (½ fl oz) extra virgin
  olive oil
4 cloves garlic, crushed
½ teaspoon chili flakes
24 large raw prawns (shrimp),
  shelled and deveined
1 medium tomato, sliced
1 cos (romaine) lettuce, outer
  leaves discarded
1 Lebanese cucumber
  (seedless), sliced into
  ribbons
salt and freshly ground black
  pepper
juice of 1 lime
juice of 1 lemon

METHOD

- Heat a large heavy-based frypan, add the oil, garlic, chili flakes and prawns. Cook, stirring constantly, until the prawns change colour, about 3 minutes.
- Divide the tomato slices between 4 serving plates, top with lettuces leaves and cucumber ribbons. Add the prawns and pour over the pan juices. Season with salt and pepper, then squeeze over the lemon and lime juices and serve.

Barbecued Seafood Salad

SERVES 8

INGREDIENTS

30 ml (1 fl oz) lemon juice

15 ml (½ fl oz) olive oil

300 g (10½ oz) firm white
fish (swordfish, mackerel
or cod) cut into 2 cm (¾ in)
cubes

300 g (10½ oz) pink fish
(salmon, ocean trout, marlin
or tuna) cut into 2 cm (¾ in)
cubes

12 scallops

12 uncooked prawns (shrimp)
with or without shell

1 calamari (squid), cleaned
and the tube cut into rings

1 large onion, cut into rings

1 telegraph cucumber, sliced

1 bunch watercress

Raspberry and Tarragon Dressing

50 g (1½ oz) fresh tarragon

30 ml (1 fl oz) wine vinegar

30 ml (1 fl oz) lemon juice

15 ml (½ fl oz) olive oil

freshly ground black pepper

METHOD

- Place lemon juice and oil in a bowl. Whisk to combine. Add white and pink fish, scallops, prawns and calamari. Toss to combine. Cover. Marinate in the refrigerator for 1 hour or until ready to use. Do not marinate for longer than 2 hours.
- Preheat a barbecue or chargrill pan until very hot. Drain seafood mixture and place on barbecue hotplate or in pan. Add onion. Cook, turning several times, for 6–8 minutes or until seafood is just cooked. Take care not to overcook or the seafood will be tough and dry. Transfer cooked seafood to a bowl and cool, then add cucumber.
- Line a serving platter with watercress, and arrange seafood and cucumber on top.
- To make dressing, place tarragon, vinegar, lemon juice, oil and black pepper to taste in a screwtop jar. Shake to combine.
- Drizzle dressing over salad, and serve immediately.

Mains

Garlic Lobster Tails

SERVES 4

INGREDIENTS

4 lobster tails
90 g (3 oz) butter
2 cloves garlic, crushed
30 ml (1 fl oz) honey and
    lemon marinade (see below)
oil for cooking

Exotic Salad

1 avocado, cut into 5 mm
    cubes
2 Lebanese cucumbers, diced
½ small rockmelon, peeled
    and diced
60 ml (2 fl oz) honey and
    lemon marinade (see below)

Honey and Lemon
   Marinade

125 ml (4 fl oz) olive oil
30 ml (1 fl oz) lemon juice
30 ml (1 fl oz) honey
4 cloves garlic, crushed
2 bay leaves, crushed

METHOD

- With kitchen scissors, cut each side of the soft shell on the underside of the lobster tails, and remove. Run a metal skewer through the length of each tail to keep them flat while cooking. Soften the butter and mix in the garlic and honey and lemon marinade. Coat the lobster meat with the butter mixture.
- Prepare the salad before starting to cook the lobster tails. Mix the avocado, cucumber and rockmelon together. Pour the honey and lemon marinade over the salad. Refrigerate until needed.
- Heat the barbecue to medium-high and oil the grill bars. Place the lobster tails shell-side down and cook until the shell turns red. Spread with more butter mixture and turn meat-side down and cook for 5–8 minutes or until the meat turns white. Turn again and cook for 2 minutes more, shell-side down. Remove the skewers and place the lobster on warm plates. Dot with any remaining butter mixture and serve immediately with exotic salad.
- For the honey and lemon marinade, mix all ingredients together. Makes 180 ml (6 fl oz).

Prawn and Scallop Skewers

SERVES 6

INGREDIENTS

1 kg (2.2 lb) medium-size green jumbo prawns (shrimp)

12 scallops

1 red onion, cut in wedges

30 ml (1 fl oz) melted butter

90 ml (3 fl oz) sweet chili sauce

500 g (18 oz) white rice and wild rice mix

12 metal or soaked bamboo skewers

fresh coriander (cilantro) leaves, to garnish

METHOD

- Remove the prawn heads but leave the tails on. Peel and devein the prawns. Thread 2–3 prawns, 1 wedge of onion and scallops alternately onto each skewer. Brush with melted butter.
- Prepare the rice according to packet instructions. Place in heatproof dish suitable for reheating on the barbecue.
- Prepare barbecue for direct-heat cooking, heat to hot and oil the grill bars well. Place the bowl of rice at side of grill to heat. Place on the skewers and cook 2–3 minutes each side, brushing with chili sauce as they cook. If charring occurs place a sheet of baking paper onto the grill, transfer the skewers over and continue to cook until done.
- Spread the wild rice mixture on a platter and set the skewers on top. Garnish with coriander leaves. Serve immediately.

Baked Fish with Spicy Soy Sauce

SERVES 4

INGREDIENTS

1 kg (2.2 lb) whole snapper
2 teaspoons peanut oil
15 ml (½ fl oz) lemon juice
pinch of salt
1 lemon, cut into slices

Sauce

2 teaspoons peanut oil
2 cloves garlic, crushed
2 cm (¾ in) piece fresh ginger,
    grated
1 small red chili, deseeded
    and sliced
4 spring onions (scallions),
    sliced
30 ml (1 fl oz) soy sauce
15 ml (½ fl oz) kecap manis

METHOD

- Preheat oven to 200°C (400°F). Scale, gut and clean the fish (see Introduction) and pat dry. Make 2 diagonal cuts on each side of the fish. Brush fish with oil and lemon juice. Season with salt and place slices of lemon in the fish. Wrap fish up in baking paper and foil and place on a baking tray. Bake in oven for 30–40 minutes or until cooked.
- To make the sauce, heat oil in a small saucepan. Add garlic, ginger, chili and spring onions and cook for 1–2 minutes. Add soy sauce, kecap manis and 125 ml (4 fl oz) water and cook for 2–3 minutes.
- When fish is cooked, transfer to a large serving dish and pour sauce over. Serve with side bowls of boiled rice.

Seafood Risotto

SERVES 6

INGREDIENTS

1 kg (2.2 lb) marinara mix
(oysters, scallops, prawns
(shrimp), crayfish, all
shelled)

125 ml (4 fl oz) olive oil

1 medium onion, chopped

2 cloves garlic, chopped

650 g (23 oz) arborio rice

1 bunch spring onions,
chopped

1 bunch fresh coriander
(cilantro), chopped

1 medium pumpkin, chopped
into small chunks

1.5 L (3 pints) fish stock

250 ml (8 fl oz) dry white wine

175 g (6 oz) Parmesan
cheese, grated

salt and freshly ground black
pepper, to taste

45 ml (1½ fl oz) sour cream

METHOD

- Wash and dry marinara mix and set aside.
- Heat oil in a large saucepan and gently fry onion and garlic. When onion is translucent, add rice. Stir well, until rice is coated with oil. Add spring onions and coriander and cook for a few minutes, then add pumpkin.
- Add 250 ml (8 fl oz) stock, stirring constantly until liquid is absorbed into the rice. Add wine and continue to stir. Continue to add stock by the cupful and stir regularly, until all stock is absorbed. It will take about 30 minutes to get the rice to an almost cooked stage.
- When rice is almost cooked, fold in the marinara mix and cook for a further 5 minutes. Add some of the Parmesan. Season with salt and pepper. Cook for another few minutes, until seafood is done, then stir in sour cream.
- Serve in bowls, and sprinkle the last of the Parmesan on top.

Deep-Fried Fish

SERVES 4

INGREDIENTS

4 fillets of fish
(shark, whiting, garfish,
   flathead, snapper, mulloway,
   trevally, cod or trout)

Batter

250 g (8 oz) plain flour
pinch of salt
60 g (2 oz) melted butter
2 eggs, lightly beaten
250 ml (8 fl oz) beer
1 egg white, stiffly beaten
extra plain flour, for coating
   fish
olive oil, for frying
lemon wedges to garnish
tartare sauce

METHOD

- To make the batter, combine flour, salt, butter and eggs. Gradually add beer and stir until smooth. Cover and stand for one hour in a warm place. Just before using, fold in egg white (this makes a light, fluffy batter). Flour fish and coat with batter.
- To deep-fry fish, heat enough oil to cover fish in a deep frypan or electric fryer. Test temperature by putting a 2.5 cm (1 in) cube of bread in the pan – it should brown in one minute when the oil is at the correct temperature. Place coated fish in oil, avoiding contact between pieces. Cook fish for about five minutes. Drain well on absorbent paper.
- Serve piping hot with lemon wedges and tartare sauce.

Seafood Casserole

SERVES 4—6

INGREDIENTS

15 ml (½ fl oz) olive oil
1 medium onion, roughly chopped
1 leek, finely chopped
2 cloves garlic, crushed
500 g (18 oz) canned tomatoes
2 bay leaves
1 tablespoon chopped fresh parsley
60 ml (2 fl oz) dry white wine
salt and freshly ground black pepper
1 kg (2.2 lb) assorted fish and seafood
2 tablespoons chopped fresh oregano to garnish

METHOD

- Heat the oil in a frypan, add onion, leek and garlic and cook for 5 minutes until softened.
- Transfer to a slow cooker set on high and add the tomatoes, bay leaves, parsley, wine, salt and pepper. Bring to the simmer, cover and cook for 50 minutes.
- Stir in any firm-fleshed fish and cook for 25 minutes.
- Stir in the soft-fleshed fish, placing the shellfish on the top. Cover with a lid and continue cooking for 40 minutes (until the fish is tender).
- Serve garnished with the oregano.

- Note: Suitable fish and seafood include red mullet, monkfish, sea bream, cod, calamari, mussels, shelled prawns (shrimp) and clams.

Singapore Chili Crab

INGREDIENTS

2 raw mud crabs, weighing
  about 1 kg (2.2 lb) each
30 ml (1 fl oz) sambal oelek
  (chili paste)
180 (6 fl oz) tomato sauce
90 ml (3 fl oz) chili sauce
30 ml (1 fl oz) oyster sauce
15 g (½ oz) sugar
1 teaspoon salt
15 ml (½ fl oz) vegetable oil
6 cloves garlic, minced
500 ml (1 pint) hot chicken
  stock
2 egg whites
60 g (2 oz) coriander
  (cilantro) leaves

METHOD

- Prepare the crab (see Introduction). Cut the body section into 4 pieces and crack the large claw shells with the back of a heavy knife. Wash the crab and drain. Scrub the back shell and keep it whole to use as a garnish.
- Combine the sambal oelek, tomato sauce and chili sauce in a small bowl. Combine the oyster sauce, sugar and salt in another.
- Heat a wok over medium-high heat and add the oil. Fry the garlic for 10 seconds, stirring constantly.
- Add the chili mixture and cook for another 10 seconds, stirring. Add the stock and oyster sauce mixture and stir again.
- Increase heat to high and bring to a fast boil. Add the crab pieces (including the back shell), stir to settle it into the liquid and cook for 3 minutes, stirring occasionally and turning the larger pieces once. Remove the back shell.
- Drizzle in the egg white and stir gently until there are white streaks through the sauce.
- Place on a serving dish, arrange the back shell on top and garnish with coriander leaves. Serve with Chinese steamed or baked buns, rice or bread and a finger bowl.

Smoked Salmon Ravioli with Lemon Dill Sauce

SERVES 4

INGREDIENTS

125 g (4 oz) smoked salmon
  pieces
1 egg white
20 ml (⅔ fl oz) cream
2 teaspoons fresh dill, roughly
  chopped
40 g (1½ oz) cornflour
  (cornstarch)
32 wonton skins
1 teaspoon oil
2–3 cups ravioli pasta

Lemon Dill Sauce

15 g (½ oz) butter
15 g (½ oz) flour
180 ml (6 fl oz) white wine
180 ml (6 fl oz) thickened
  cream
½ lemon, juiced
30 g (1 oz) dill, roughly
  chopped
salt and freshly ground
  pepper

METHOD

- Place the salmon, 15 ml (½ fl oz) of egg white, cream and dill in a food processor, and process, until well combined, like a mousse.
- Sprinkle the cornflour on a bench and lay wonton skins in rows of four.
- Brush every second skin around the edge with egg white. On alternate skins, place a teaspoon of mixture in the middle. Lie the other skin on top, gently pinch around mixture, so they look like pillows or rounds. Half-fill a large saucepan with water and oil, bring to the boil, add ravioli, cook, for 2–3 minutes. Set aside, and cover with clingwrap.
- For the lemon dill sauce, melt the butter in a saucepan, add the flour, and cook for 1 minute. Add the wine, stir until smooth, and then add the cream and lemon juice. Bring to the boil then reduce, until sauce is a pouring consistency.
- To serve, add the dill, salt and pepper to the sauce and pour over ravioli.

Seafood Paella

SERVES 8

INGREDIENTS

60 ml (2 fl oz) olive oil

30 g (1 oz) butter

2 cloves garlic, chopped

1 onion, chopped

1 capsicum (bell pepper), seeded and chopped

3 tomatoes, peeled

330 g (11½ oz) short grain rice

750 ml (1½ pints) fish stock

1 teaspoon salt

½ teaspoon saffron threads, crumbled

500 g (1.1 lb) mixture of seafood – prawns (shrimp), scallops, mussels, uncooked crab – washed, peeled, debearded and deveined

¼ teaspoon freshly ground black pepper

50 g (1¾ oz) fresh parsley, chopped

2 teaspoons fresh oregano, chopped

1 teaspoon fresh thyme, chopped

METHOD

- In a large, deep frypan (that has a lid), heat oil and butter over a medium heat.
- Add garlic, onion and capsicum, and cook until tender (about 10 minutes). Stir in tomatoes and cook for about 5 minutes. Add rice and stir, then stir in fish stock, salt and saffron.
- Cover and bring to boil, then remove lid, reduce heat and simmer for 5 minutes, stirring continually. Add seafood, then cover and simmer for a further 5 minutes. Add pepper, parsley, oregano, thyme and cook, still covered, until tender.
- Serve hot with crusty French bread.

Seafood Curry

INGREDIENTS

15 ml (½ fl oz) peanut oil

½ teaspoon ground turmeric

1 teaspoon ground coriander (cilantro)

250 ml (8 fl oz) coconut milk

30 ml (1 fl oz) lime juice

2 teaspoons palm sugar or brown sugar

2 lime leaves, shredded

400 g (14 oz) ling fillets, diced

200 g (7 oz) raw prawns (shrimp), heads removed and shelled

200 g (7 oz) squid rings

Paste

2 French shallots, chopped

2 cloves garlic, chopped

2 cm (¾ in) piece fresh ginger, chopped

3 medium chilies, deseeded and sliced

1 stalk lemongrass, very thinly sliced

½ teaspoon salt

METHOD

- Grind or pound paste ingredients in a mortar and pestle or food processor.
- Heat oil in a wok or large frypan. Add paste and cook for 1–2 minutes. Add turmeric and coriander and cook until aromatic. Add coconut milk, 60 ml (2 fl oz) water, the lime juice, palm sugar and lime leaves. Bring to the boil, add seafood and cook for 3–4 minutes or until tender.
- Serve with noodles or rice.

Fresh Crab Tagliatelle

SERVES 4

INGREDIENTS
340 g (12 oz) tagliatelle
45 ml (1½ fl oz) olive oil
2 cloves garlic, chopped
1 red chili, chopped
finely grated zest of 1 lemon
2 fresh dressed crabs, to
   give about 300 g (10½ oz)
   crabmeat
200 ml (6¾ fl oz) heavy cream
15 ml (½ fl oz) lemon juice
salt and freshly ground black
   pepper
30 g (1 oz) chopped fresh
   parsley to garnish

METHOD
- Cook the pasta in plenty of boiling salted water until tender but still firm to the bite, then drain.
- Meanwhile, heat the oil in a large, heavy-based skillet and gently fry the garlic, chili and lemon zest for 3–4 minutes until softened but not browned. Add the crabmeat, cream and lemon juice, and simmer for 1–2 minutes to heat through. Season to taste.
- Transfer the pasta to serving bowls. Spoon the crab mixture over the top and sprinkle with the parsley to garnish.

- Note: This recipe really makes the most of the fantastic flavour of fresh crab.

Barramundi Fillet

INGREDIENTS

4 x barramundi fillets
300 g (10½ oz) potatoes,
    peeled and chopped
sea salt and pepper to taste
125 ml (4 fl oz) milk

METHOD

- Trim fish and refrigerate until ready to cook.
- Peel potatoes and dice. Place in a saucepan with boiling water and boil until the potatoes are soft and cooked through. Once cooked add seasoning and a little milk and mash until creamy.
- Heat the grill to medium hot. Spray both side of the fish with vegetable oil and cook on the grill until each piece of fish is cooked through depending on thickness of fillet. The fish will turn a firm white.
- Place fish on individual plates with potato mash and serve with greens of your choice.

Cod with Basil Aioli

SERVES 4

INGREDIENTS

1 clove garlic, minced

30 ml (1 fl oz) olive oil

15 ml (½ fl oz) lemon juice

4 cod cutlets, or other firm
    white fish

Basil Aioli

4 medium cloves garlic

½ teaspoon sea salt

2 egg yolks

½ teaspoon lemon juice

125 g (4 oz) fresh basil

125 ml (4 fl oz) olive oil

METHOD

- Combine the garlic, olive oil and lemon juice in a dish and marinate the fish cutlets for 1 hour.
- For the basil aioli put the garlic, salt, egg yolks, lemon juice and basil into the food processor and blend for 30 seconds.
- When this mixture is starting to thicken, slowly pour the oil down the feeder shoot. As it takes, you can add the oil a little more quickly until finished. Use immediately or store for up to five days.
- Grease a hinged wire basket and place the fish inside. Preheat the barbecue and place the basket over the grill. Grill the fish for 3 minutes on each side.
- Serve immediately with the basil aioli.

Coriander Swordfish Steaks

SERVES 4

INGREDIENTS

4 swordfish steaks

15 ml (½ fl oz) olive oil

4 zucchini, cut into long slices

1 red capsicum (bell pepper),
 quartered

125 g (4 oz) unsalted butter

60 g (2 oz) coriander
 (cilantro), chopped

40 g (1½ oz) Parmesan
 cheese, grated

METHOD

- Heat the barbecue grill until hot and brush with oil. Brush the fish steaks with oil, place on the grill bars and cook for 3–4 minutes each side according to thickness. Brush or spray the vegetables with oil and place on the grill. Cook a few minutes on each side. Remove the fish steaks and vegetables to heated plates.
- Cream the butter until soft and mix in the coriander and parmesan. Top the swordfish steaks with a generous dollop of the coriander butter mixture and serve immediately.

Spaghetti with Mussels

SERVES 4

INGREDIENTS

2 kg (4.4 lb) mussels

125 ml (4 fl oz) extra virgin olive oil

350 g (12 oz) spaghetti

100 ml (3½ fl oz) dry white wine

60 g (2 oz) chopped fresh parsley

2 cloves garlic, chopped

1 teaspoon crushed dried chilies

METHOD

- Scrub the mussels under cold running water, pull away any beards and discard any mussels that are open or damaged. Place 2 tablespoons of the oil in a large, heavy-based skillet, then add the mussels. Cook, covered, shaking the skillet frequently for 2–4 minutes or until the mussels open. Discard any mussels that do not open.
- Reserve 12 mussels in their shells for garnishing. Detach the remaining mussels from their shells and set aside. Discard the shells.
- Cook the pasta in plenty of boiling salted water until tender but still firm to the bite, then drain.
- Meanwhile, place the remaining oil, the wine, parsley, garlic and chili in a large, heavy-based skillet and bring to the boil. Cook for 2 minutes to boil off the alcohol. Stir the mussels and pasta into the oil and chili mixture and toss for 30 seconds to heat through. Serve garnished with the reserved mussels.

Pad Thai

SERVES 4

INGREDIENTS

350 g (12 oz) fresh or dried
  rice noodles
2 teaspoons vegetable oil
4 French shallots (scallions),
  chopped
3 fresh red chilies, chopped
8 cm (3 in) piece fresh ginger,
  grated
250 g (8 oz) medium raw
  prawns (shrimp), shelled
  and deveined
50 g (1¾ oz) roasted peanuts,
  chopped
15 g (½ oz) sugar
60 ml (2 fl oz) lime juice
45 ml (1½ fl oz) fish sauce
30 ml (1 fl oz) light soy sauce
125 g (4 oz) tofu, chopped
50 g (1¾ oz) bean sprouts
125 g (4 oz) coriander
  (cilantro) leaves
125 g (4 oz) mint leaves
1 lime, cut into wedges

METHOD

- Place noodles in a bowl and pour over boiling water to cover. If using fresh noodles soak for 2 minutes; if using dried noodles soak for 5–6 minutes or until soft. Drain well and set aside.
- Heat oil in a frypan or wok over a high heat, add shallots, chilies and ginger, and stir-fry for 1 minute. Add prawns, and stir-fry for 4 minutes or until cooked.
- Add noodles, peanuts, sugar, lime juice and fish and soy sauces and stir-fry for 4 minutes or until heated through.
- Stir in tofu, bean sprouts, coriander and mint, and cook for 1–2 minutes.
- Serve with lime wedges.

Mussels Tin Tin

SERVES 4

INGREDIENTS

60 ml (2 fl oz) white wine
1 red chili, sliced
1 stalk lemongrass, bruised
4 cm (1½ in) piece ginger,
  chopped
1 clove garlic, chopped
1 kg (2.2 lb) mussels, cleaned
15 ml (¼ fl oz) peanut oil
125 ml (4 fl oz) coconut
  cream
60 g (2 oz) coriander
  (cilantro), chopped

METHOD

- Put white wine, chili, lemongrass, ginger and garlic in a pot and infuse together for 15 minutes.
- Put mussels in a casserole dish with oil, and add the infusion.
- Add coconut cream and cook until mussels have opened, stirring frequently. Discard the lemongrass and any mussels that do not open. Stir in coriander and serve.

Char Kway Teow (Fried Noodles)

SERVES 4

INGREDIENTS

300 g (10½ oz) thick, flat rice
   noodles
2 teaspoons sambal oelek
   (chili paste)
4 teaspoons kecap manis
4 teaspoons light soy sauce
4 teaspoons oyster sauce
30 ml (1 fl oz) vegetable oil
12 large raw prawns (shrimp),
   peeled
1 squid tube, cut into strips
4 cloves garlic, minced
4 eggs
1 large handful bean sprouts
100g (3½ oz) clam meat

METHOD

- Cover the noodles with boiling water, leave for 15 minutes, then drain. Combine the chili paste, kecap manis and sauces in a small bowl.
- Heat a wok over medium-high heat and add the oil. Add the shrimp and squid and stir-fry for about 10 seconds. Add the garlic and fry for another 10 seconds, stirring constantly.
- Crack in the eggs and stir gently until just cooked. Add the noodles and stir briefly. Add the combined sauces.
- Increase heat to high and stir-fry until the noodles are coated with sauce. Add the bean sprouts and clam meat and stir through.
- Splash 60 ml (2 fl oz) water in around the sides of the wok and stir-fry for about 15 seconds or until well combined but not too dry. Serve immediately.

Piri Piri-Spiced Prawns

SERVES 4

INGREDIENTS

1 kg (2.2 lb) medium raw
   prawns (shrimp)
15 ml (½ fl oz) peanut oil
30 ml (1 fl oz) lemon juice
2 teaspoons piri piri
   seasoning
2 teaspoons parsley flakes
1 clove garlic, freshly crushed
125 g (4 oz) plain flour
vegetable oil for deep-frying

METHOD

- Remove the heads and shells from the prawns, leaving the tails intact. Using a sharp knife, make an incision along the back of the prawns, remove the vein and cut into the shrimp so it opens out.
- Combine the peanut oil, lemon juice, piri piri seasoning, parsley and garlic in a bowl. Add the shrimp and coat in the mixture. Dip the shrimp lightly in the flour.
- Heat the oil in a wok or frypan. Cook the shrimp in batches for 1–2 minutes or until golden and crisp.
- Serve the shrimp with lime wedges.

Fish Fingers

SERVES 2

INGREDIENTS

500 g (1.1 lb) boneless fish
    fillets
125 g (4 oz) potato starch
30 g (1 oz) egg replacer
250 g (8 oz) fine rice crumbs

METHOD

- Mince the fish fillets and press the meat into an ice-block tray. Freeze for at least 2 hours, or overnight.
- Place the potato starch in a plastic bag and beat the egg replacer with 125 g (4 oz) warm water until well mixed.
- Take the frozen fish blocks one at a time, toss in the potato starch, then dip in the egg replacer and then in the rice crumbs. Fry in a small amount of oil until golden, or bake in the oven for about 20 minutes from frozen. Place any leftovers on a tray to refreeze, then pack in user-friendly packs for future use.
- To make these fish fingers you will need a mincer, or you can finely chop the fish and moisten it with a little of the egg replacer.

Spaghetti Vongole

INGREDIENTS

300 g (10½ oz) spaghetti

45 ml (1½ fl oz) virgin olive oil

1 onion, very finely chopped

2 cloves garlic, finely chopped

500 g (1.1 lb) clams, cleaned and sand removed

125 ml (4 fl oz) white wine

salt and freshly ground black pepper

60 g (2 oz) fresh oregano, chopped

METHOD

- Bring a large saucepan of salted water to the boil, add the pasta and cook for 8 minutes or until just firm in the centre (al dente). Refresh in cold water, stir with half the oil and set aside.
- Heat the remaining oil in a large cooking pot over high heat. Add the onion and garlic and cook for 1 minute.
- Add the clams, white wine, salt and pepper.
- When all the clams have opened, add the spaghetti and oregano. Cook for another 2 minutes, then serve.

San Franciscan Seafood Chowder in Bread Cups

SERVES 8

INGREDIENTS

8 small round loaves of bread
90 g (3 oz) butter
2 leeks, finely sliced
2 onions, finely chopped
4 cloves garlic, minced
2 carrots, peeled and
    chopped
1 parsnip, peeled and
    chopped
2 stalks celery, finely sliced
4 sprigs thyme, leaves
    removed and stalks
    discarded
60 g (2 oz) plain flour
2 L (4¼ pints) fish stock
1 kg (2.2 lb) mixed seafood
    including prawns (shrimp),
    mussels, clams, squid and
    white fish
180 ml (6 fl oz) thickened
    cream
½ bunch parsley, chopped
salt and freshly ground black
    pepper
juice of 1 large lemon
½ bunch chives, chopped

METHOD

- Preheat the oven to 200°C (400°F). Using a sharp knife, cut a large hole in the top of each bread loaf, then remove crusty top and set aside. Carefully remove all soft bread from inside of loaves, leaving the surrounding crust intact. Bake for 15 minutes until the loaves are crisp and dry. Set aside.
- Melt butter in a large saucepan and add leeks, onions, garlic, carrots, parsnip, celery and thyme. Sauté for 10 minutes until soft and golden. Remove the saucepan from the heat and sprinkle flour over vegetables, stirring constantly to mix the flour with butter. Return the saucepan to the heat and continue stirring until the mixture begins to turn golden, about 2 minutes.
- Add fish stock, stirring constantly, then simmer the chowder for 20 minutes. Meanwhile, cut the seafood into bite-size pieces.
- Add all the seafood and the cream, parsley and salt and pepper, and cook for a further 5 minutes. Do not allow the chowder to boil rapidly because it may curdle. Once the shellfish has cooked, stir lemon juice through the chowder, then ladle into the bread cups. Garnish with chopped chives and serve.

Seafood Rice
with Chili Lime Butter

SERVES 4

INGREDIENTS

250 g (8 oz) basmati rice

16 large raw prawns (shrimp)

2 teaspoons olive oil

100 g (3½ oz) butter, melted

1 red chili, finely sliced

1 green chili, finely sliced

1 small red onion, finely sliced

1 lime, peeled and cut into
   small dice

juice of 1 lime

125 g (4 oz) fresh coriander
   (cilantro), chopped

METHOD

- Combine the rice with 500 ml (1 pint) water in a saucepan. Bring to the boil, reduce heat to low, cover and cook for 15 minutes, then allow to stand covered for 10 minutes.
- Shell the shrimp, leaving the tails intact. To butterfly the shrimp, cut along the back, about halfway through. Remove the vein.
- Heat the oil in a heavy-based frying pan, add the shrimp and cook until they change colour and are just cooked through. Set aside and keep warm.
- Return pan to heat, add butter, chili and onion. Sauté for 1–2 minutes, then add cooked rice and chopped lime and mix well. Add prawns, season with lime juice, stir through coriander and serve.

Grilled Snapper with Cucumber, Radish and Beetroot Salad

SERVES 4

INGREDIENTS

4 snapper fillets, about 250 g (8 oz) each

3 cm (1.2 in) piece fresh ginger

60 ml (2 fl oz) mirin

30 ml (1 fl oz) lime juice

1 lime, thinly sliced

Cucumber, Radish and Beetroot Salad

3 cucumbers, peeled

1 small fresh daikon radish, peeled

2 fresh beetroots

¼ teaspoon wasabi paste

60 ml (2 fl oz) rice wine vinegar

30 ml (1 fl oz) peanut oil

METHOD

- Preheat the barbecue. Place the snapper in the centre of 4 large pieces of baking paper. Peel the ginger, slice and cut into thin strips. Combine 30 ml (1 fl oz) of the mirin, lime juice and ginger in a bowl. Spoon lime juice mixture over the fish and divide the lime slices between fillets.
- Wrap the fillets up to form 4 parcels, tucking the sides under. Place the parcels on the grill and barbecue for 10–15 minutes, or until cooked through.
- To make the salad, cut the cucumbers in half lengthways and scrape out the seeds. Cut pieces in half and then into matchstick-size pieces. Cut the daikon into 8 cm (3 in) long pieces, then into thin slices by hand or on a mandolin. Stack the slices and cut into matchstick-size pieces. Thinly slice the beetroot by hand or on a mandolin, stack the slices and cut into matchstick-size pieces.
- Place the vegetables in a bowl and toss. Combine the remaining mirin, wasabi, vinegar and oil to make a dressing and pour over the vegetables just before serving, or serve dressing separately. Serve the salad with the snapper parcels.

Oriental-style Salmon Fillets

SERVES 4

INGREDIENTS

4 skinless salmon fillets

30 ml (1 fl oz) vegetable oil

30 ml (1 fl oz) light soy sauce

30 ml (1 fl oz) honey

30 g (1 oz) preserved ginger,
   drained and finely chopped

2 spring onions (scallions),
   cut into long strips

finely grated zest and juice of
   1 lime

freshly ground black pepper

METHOD

- Place the salmon fillets in a shallow non-metallic dish. Mix together the oil, soy sauce, honey, ginger, spring onions, lime zest and juice and seasoning. Pour over the fillets and turn to coat. Cover and marinate in the refrigerator for 10 minutes, or 1 hour if you have time.
- Preheat the barbecue. Lightly oil four large pieces of baking paper and place the fillets and spring onions in the centre. Fold the baking paper to form a parcel and tuck the edges underneath.
- Place the parcels on the grill and leave to cook for 5 minutes. Turn over, and cook for 3–5 minutes, or until the fish is cooked through.

Tuna Niçoise

SERVES 8

INGREDIENTS

170 g (6 oz) green beans, cut
    into 8 cm (3 in) lengths
60 ml (2 fl oz) olive oil
4 tuna steaks, about 170 g
    (6 oz) each and 2.5 cm (1
    in) thick
salt and freshly ground black
    pepper
1 red capsicum (bell pepper),
    deseeded and diced
12 cherry tomatoes, halved
16 black olives, pitted
15 ml (¼ fl oz) balsamic
    vinegar
60 g (2 oz) flat-leaf parsley

METHOD

- Cook beans in boiling salted water for 3–5 minutes, until tender but still firm to the bite. Drain, refresh under cold water and set aside. Place 30 ml (1 fl oz) of oil in a shallow bowl, add tuna and turn to coat, then season lightly.
- Heat a large heavy-based frying pan over a high heat, then add tuna and cook for 1 minute on each side. Reduce the heat and cook for a further 1–2 minutes on each side, until steaks have browned slightly. Set aside.
- Heat remaining oil in the frying pan and fry the red capsicum for 1 minute or until softened. Add the beans, tomatoes and olives and stir-fry for 1 minute to warm through. Remove from the pan, pour in vinegar, and use it to deglaze the pan. Serve tuna topped with the capsicum mixture and parsley, then drizzle the vinegar mixture.

Tuna Fish Cakes

SERVES 4

INGREDIENTS

4 slices bread, crusts removed
700g (1lb 8oz) floury potatoes, halved or quartered depending on size
50 g (1¾ oz) mayonnaise
400 g (14 oz) canned tuna in oil, drained and flaked
¼ cup dill, chopped
2 spring onions (scallions), finely chopped
finely grated zest of 1 small lemon
50 g (1¾ oz) plain flour
1 medium egg, beaten
vegetable oil for frying

METHOD

- Preheat the oven to 160°C (325°F). Place the bread on a baking sheet and cook at the bottom of the oven for 20–30 minutes until crisp. Cool, break into pieces and crush with a rolling pin.
- Meanwhile, cook the potatoes in a large saucepan of boiling salted water for 15 minutes or until tender. Drain, transfer to a bowl and mash with the mayonnaise. Leave to cool for 30 minutes.
- Mash the tuna, dill, spring onions and lemon zest into the potatoes. Flour your hands, then shape the mixture into 8 flat cakes. Dust with flour and dip into the egg, then into the breadcrumbs.
- Heat 5 mm (⅕ in) of oil in a large heavy-based frying pan and cook the fish cakes for 3–4 minutes on each side until crisp and golden (you may have to cook them in batches). Drain on absorbent paper, then serve with the lemon wedges.

- Note: These chunky fish cakes are packed with flavour and it only takes a few vegetables or a salad to make a complete meal. Canned salmon works just as well as the tuna.

Tuna Seviche

INGREDIENTS

500 g (17½ oz) tuna steaks, diced

½ small red onion, thinly sliced

30 ml (1 fl oz) extra virgin olive oil

250 ml (8 fl oz) lime juice

1 teaspoon Dijon mustard

¼ teaspoon sugar

2 cloves garlic, crushed

1 long red chili, deseeded and finely chopped

salt and freshly ground black pepper

15 g (½ oz) roughly chopped roasted peanuts

2 spring onions, sliced

60 g (2 oz) coriander (cilantro), freshly chopped

METHOD

- Place fish and red onion in a ceramic dish.
- Whisk together olive oil, lime juice, Dijon mustard, sugar, garlic and chili in a jug.
- Pour over fish and toss well. Season with salt and pepper.
- Cover with cling wrap and refrigerate for 1 hour.
- Sprinkle with peanuts, spring onions and coriander and serve with lime wedges.

Salmon with Onion and Red Wine

SERVES 4

INGREDIENTS

125 ml (4 fl oz) red wine

½ small red onion, finely chopped

75 g (2½ oz) butter, at room temperature

60 g (2 oz) fresh parsley, finely chopped

1 clove garlic, very finely chopped

sea salt and freshly ground black pepper

15 ml (½ fl oz) sunflower oil

4 salmon fillets, about 175 g (6 oz) each, skinned

METHOD

- Place the wine and onion in a small saucepan and bring to the boil. Boil rapidly for about 4–5 minutes over a high heat or until reduced to about 30 ml (1 fl oz). Remove from the heat and allow to cool completely.
- In a bowl, beat the butter until smooth, add the parsley, garlic, seasoning and reduced wine and mix together with a fork. Place the butter in cling wrap on a piece of baking paper and roll up into a tight sausage shape. Refrigerate until hardened.
- Heat the oil in a large frying pan over a medium heat and cook the salmon for 4 minutes. Turn and cook for 3–4 minutes more, until cooked through. Cut the butter into four pieces, place one on top of each salmon fillet, and cook for 2 minutes more before serving.

Teriyaki Fish Fillets

SERVES 4

INGREDIENTS

4 boneless white fish fillets,
    about 180 g (6 oz) each
250 ml (8 fl oz) bought
    teriyaki marinade (see note)
15 ml (½ fl oz) lemon juice
1 bunch bok choy, trimmed
    and separated

Teriyaki Sauce

250 ml (8 fl oz) bought
    teriyaki marinade (see note)
250 ml (8 fl oz) water
½ teaspoon chili flakes
2 spring onions (scallions),
    sliced

METHOD

- Preheat the oven to 180°C (350°F).
- Brush the fish fillets with the marinade. Place on sheets of foil and drizzle each fillet with 1 teaspoon lemon juice. Wrap the fish in foil and place on a baking tray. Bake for 10–15 minutes or until cooked. Remove the fish from the foil and pour any juice from the fish into the sauce.
- Boil or steam the bok choy until bright green.
- To make the teriyaki sauce, combine all the ingredients and juice from the fish in a small saucepan. Bring to the boil, reduce the heat to low and simmer for 1 minute.
- Serve the fish fillets on a bed of steamed bok choy and spoon over teriyaki sauce.

- Note If you would prefer to make your own teriyaki marinade, heat all the following ingredients in a pan, stir to combine, then allow to cool: 125 ml (4 fl oz) soy sauce, 30 g (1 oz) brown sugar, ½ teaspoon ground ginger, 30 ml (1 fl oz) white wine vinegar, 1 teaspoon crushed garlic, 30 ml (1 fl oz) tomato sauce.

Pan-Fried Fish (Ikan Goreng)

SERVES 4

INGREDIENTS

15 ml (½ fl oz) peanut oil
4 boneless fish fillets
250 ml (8 fl oz) coconut milk
1 teaspoon palm sugar or
  brown sugar
15 ml (½ fl oz) lemon juice
4 green shallots, sliced

Paste

2 cloves garlic, chopped
2 teaspoons root ginger,
  chopped
1 stalk lemongrass, sliced
2 medium chilies, deseeded
  and sliced
2 candle nuts
1 teaspoon terasi
1 teaspoon ground coriander
  (cilantro)
2 teaspoons peanut oil

METHOD

- Grind or pound paste ingredients in a mortar with pestle or a food processor. Brush paste over fish fillets.
- Heat remaining oil in a large frying pan. Add fish fillets and cook for 1–2 minutes on each side. Add coconut milk, sugar and lemon juice and simmer for 2–3 minutes. Serve fish topped with green shallots.

- Note: Macadamia nuts may be substituted for candle nuts.

Poached Salmon and Citrus Rice

SERVES 4

INGREDIENTS

250 g (8 oz) brown rice

zest and juice of 1 lemon

125 g (4 oz) parsley, finely
  chopped

4 salmon fillets, about 200 g
  (7 oz) each

1 carrot, cut into matchsticks

1 stalk celery, cut into thin
  strips

1 green capsicum (bell
  pepper), cut into thin strips

salt and freshly ground black
  pepper

60 ml (2 fl oz) white wine

small bunch dill, roughly
  chopped

METHOD

- Preheat oven to 200°C (400°F).
- Combine the rice with 2 cups water in a saucepan. Bring to the boil, reduce heat to low, cover and cook for 15 minutes. Remove pan from heat, stir through lemon juice and parsley. Stand covered for 10 minutes.
- Meanwhile, place the salmon portions on a single sheet of baking paper. Top with lemon zest and finely sliced vegetables, season with salt and pepper and drizzle with white wine. Fold the sides of the baking paper together to form a tight parcel. Bake for 10–12 minutes.
- Remove salmon from the parcel, top with baked vegetables and dill. Carefully pour over juices that have collected in the bag. Serve with citrus rice.

Lemon and Dill Salmon with Spinach

SERVES 4

INGREDIENTS

4 salmon fillets, about 250 g (9 oz) each

15 g (½ oz) lemon and dill seasoning

salt and freshly ground black pepper

45 ml (1½ fl oz) olive oil

750 g (1 lb 10 oz) desiree potatoes, thinly sliced

250 ml (8 fl oz) chicken stock

1 bunch English spinach, washed and trimmed

1 lemon, cut into wedges

METHOD

- Place the salmon fillets on a plate and sprinkle both sides evenly with lemon and dill seasoning and pepper. Press lightly to coat.
- Heat 1 tablespoon oil in a large frying pan on medium-to-high heat. Add the salmon fillets, skin-side down, and cook for 3 minutes or until the skin is golden and crisp. Turn the fillets and cook for a further 2–3 minutes or until cooked to your liking. Remove and keep warm.
- Heat the remaining oil in a large frying pan. Add the potato slices and cook in batches for 1–2 minutes on each side or until just golden. Add the stock, return the remaining potatoes to the pan and simmer for 4–5 minutes or until tender. Add the spinach, season with salt and pepper, and cook until the spinach wilts.
- Serve the salmon on a bed of potatoes and spinach with pan juices and lemon wedges.

- Note You can vary this dish by using ocean trout fillets or salmon cutlets. The best way to serve salmon is to undercook it a little so it is pink inside. Cooking times for salmon will vary depending on the thickness of the fillet.

Red Snapper with Coconut Sauce

SERVES 4

INGREDIENTS

600 g (1 lb 5 oz) red snapper
2 stalks lemongrass, very
  finely sliced
2 cm (¾ in) piece galangal,
  grated
6 cloves garlic, roughly
  chopped
1 French shallot, roughly
  chopped
2 small red chilies, deseeded
2 kaffir lime leaves
60 g (2 oz) dill
15 g (½ oz) sesame seeds

Coconut Sauce

500 ml (1 pint) coconut milk
juice of 2 limes
30 g (1 oz) palm sugar
15 ml (½ fl oz) fish sauce

METHOD

- Combine all ingredients except snapper in a food processor and blend to a smooth paste.
- Divide fish into four even portions. Remove any major bones. Score skin of fish with a sharp knife.
- Smear paste onto snapper, pressing into slits. Set aside for cooking.
- Prepare coconut sauce by combining coconut milk, lime juice, palm sugar and fish sauce in a small saucepan. Heat until warm and sugar has dissolved.
- Heat a little oil in a frying pan until almost smoking and add fish, skin-side down. Cook until golden brown, about 2 minutes on each side.
- Serve with coconut sauce and Asian greens.

Chinese-Style Steamed Grey Mullet

SERVES 4

INGREDIENTS

2 grey mullet, about 680 g
(1 lb 6 oz) each

2 teaspoons salt

30 ml (1 fl oz) vegetable oil

30 ml (1 fl oz) light soy sauce

1 large carrot, cut into fine
strips

8 spring onions (scallions),
cut into fine strips

8 cm (3 in) piece fresh ginger,
grated

30 ml (1 fl oz) sesame oil

60 g (2 oz) fresh coriander
(cilantro) leaves

METHOD

- Scale and gut the mullet (see Introduction), then clean and pat dry. Make 4 deep slashes along each side of the fish, then rub the fish inside and out with salt, vegetable oil and soy sauce. Cover and place in the refrigerator for 30 minutes.
- Spread half the carrot, spring onions and ginger on a large piece of foil. Place fish on top, then sprinkle with remaining vegetables and ginger and any remaining marinade. Loosely fold over foil to seal. Transfer fish to a steamer.
- Cook for 20 minutes or until the fish is firm and cooked through. Heat sesame oil in a small saucepan, drizzle over fish and garnish with coriander.

Grilled Sardines

SERVES 4

INGREDIENTS

12 sardines, cleaned

60 ml (2 fl oz) extra virgin
   olive oil

sea salt

1 lemon, cut into wedges

Salad

1 green capsicum (bell
   pepper)

1 yellow capsicum (bell
   pepper)

3 tomatoes, diced

1 red onion, diced

30 ml (1 fl oz) extra virgin
olive oil

15 ml (½ fl oz) white wine
   vinegar

½ teaspoon sugar

salt and freshly ground black
   pepper

METHOD

- Place sardines in a large shallow ceramic dish. Drizzle with olive oil and sprinkle over salt, cover with cling wrap and refrigerate for 1–2 hours.
- Preheat a grill or barbecue. Cook sardines for 3–4 minutes each side or until golden and cooked.
- To make salad, cut green and yellow capsicum in four and remove seeds.
- Place on a baking tray under a hot grill for 6–8 minutes or until skin blisters. Leave to cool, then remove skin and dice. Toss together capsicum, tomatoes, onion, olive oil, vinegar, sugar, salt and pepper.
- Serve sardines with lemon wedges and the salad.

Pan-Fried Squid with Lemon

SERVES 4

INGREDIENTS

680 g (1 lb 6 oz) squid tubes

125 g (4 oz) fine semolina

1 teaspoon salt

1 teaspoon freshly ground
black pepper

250 (8 fl oz) olive oil

1 lemon, cut into wedges

METHOD

- Cut each squid tube along 1 side. With a sharp knife, score inside skin diagonally in both directions, making a diamond pattern. Cut squid into 2 x 4 cm (¾ x 1½ in) rectangles.
- In a bowl, combine semolina, salt and pepper.
- Heat oil in a large frying pan or wok until hot. Dip squid into semolina and cook in batches until lightly brown and crisp. Drain on absorbent paper and serve with lemon wedges.

Lobster Provençale

INGREDIENTS

60 g (2 oz) butter
1 large clove garlic, crushed
2 spring onions (scallions),
  chopped
300 g (10½ oz) canned
  tomatoes
salt and freshly ground black
  pepper
pinch of saffron threads
1 large lobster, cooked
45 ml (1½ fl oz) brandy
750 g (24 oz) boiled rice
½ bunch chives, chopped

METHOD

- In a shallow frying pan, melt butter over a moderate heat. Add garlic, spring onions, tomatoes, salt, pepper and saffron. Cook until onions are translucent, about 2 minutes.
- Remove meat from lobster and cut into large pieces. Add lobster to frying pan and flame with the brandy. Cook gently until lobster is heated through.
- Place rice on serving plate and sprinkle with chives.
- Remove lobster from frying pan, retaining the cooking liquid as a sauce.
- Arrange the lobster on the rice and spoon the cooking liquid over lobster. Serve with lemon wedges.

Scampi with Basil Butter

SERVES 4

INGREDIENTS

8 raw scampi or yabbies,
  heads removed

Basil Butter

90 g (3 oz) butter, melted
60 g (2 oz) fresh basil,
  chopped
1 clove garlic, crushed
2 teaspoons honey

METHOD

- Cut scampi or yabbies in half lengthwise.
- To make basil butter, place butter, basil, garlic and honey in a small bowl and whisk to combine.
- Brush each cut side of scampi or yabbie with basil butter and cook under a preheated hot grill for 2 minutes or until they change colour and are tender. Drizzle with any remaining basil butter and serve immediately.

Lobster Mornay

SERVES 4

INGREDIENTS

2 medium lobsters, cooked
   and halved

Mornay Sauce

300 ml (10 fl oz) milk

1 bay leaf

1 small onion, chopped

5 black peppercorns

30 g (1 oz) butter, plus 15 g
   (½ oz)

30 g (1 oz) plain flour

60 ml (2 fl oz) cream

65 g (2 oz) cheddar cheese,
   grated

salt and freshly ground black
   pepper

65 g (2 oz) fresh breadcrumbs

METHOD

- Remove the lobster meat from the shells and cut into bite-size pieces. Reserve the shells.
- In a saucepan, place the milk, bay leaf, onion and peppercorns. Heat slowly to boiling point. Remove from the heat, cover and stand for 10 minutes. Strain.
- In a pan, melt 30 g (1 oz) butter, then remove from the heat. Stir in the flour and blend, gradually adding the strained milk. Return the pan to the heat, and stir constantly until the sauce boils and thickens. Simmer for 1 minute, remove from the heat, add the cream, cheese, salt and pepper. Stir the sauce until the cheese melts, then add the lobster.
- Divide the mixture between the shells. Melt the remaining butter in a small pan, add the breadcrumbs, and stir to combine. Scatter the crumbs over the lobster and brown under a hot grill.

Snapper Fillets with White Wine and Parsley

SERVES 4

INGREDIENTS

125 g (4 oz) plain flour

1 teaspoon coarse ground pepper

¼ teaspoon sea salt

4 snapper fillets, 250 g (8 oz) each

30 ml (1 fl oz) olive oil

60 g (2 oz) butter

2 cloves garlic, crushed

125 ml (4 fl oz) white wine

30 g (1 oz) parsley, finely chopped

METHOD

- Combine the flour, pepper and salt in a dish, and coat the fish fillets evenly with flour, shaking off any excess.
- Heat the barbecue to a medium heat, place the fish on the grill and cook gently for 5–6 minutes on each side, depending on the thickness of fish. Set the fish aside on a plate, and keep warm.
- Melt the butter in a pan, add the garlic and cook for 2 minutes. Add the white wine and simmer, until the sauce reduces.
- Just before serving, add the chopped parsley to the sauce and then pour over the fish.

Spiced Fish Kebabs

SERVES 4

INGREDIENTS

750 g (1 lb 8 oz) firm white
   fish fillets, cut into 25 mm
   (1 in) cubes
oil for cooking
15 g (½ oz) ground paprika
1 teaspoon crushed black
   peppercorns
1 teaspoon ground cummin
½ teaspoon chili powder

Lemon Yoghurt Sauce

125 ml (4 fl oz) low-fat natural
   yoghurt
15 ml (½ fl oz) lemon juice
60 g (2 oz) thyme or lemon
   thyme, chopped
freshly ground black pepper

METHOD

- Thread fish onto lightly oiled skewers. Place the paprika, black pepper, cummin and chili powder in a bowl and mix to combine. Sprinkle the spice mixture over the kebabs.
- Cook the kebabs on a preheated barbecue for 2–3 minutes each side or until the fish is cooked.
- To make the sauce, place the yoghurt, lemon juice, thyme and black pepper in a bowl and mix to combine. Serve with the kebabs.

Barbecued Fish Burger

SERVES 4

INGREDIENTS

4 cod fillets, or other firm white fish approximately 125 g (4 oz) each

60 ml (2 fl oz) Thai-style seafood seasoning

4 round Turkish pide

90 g (3 oz) butter, softened

200 g (7 oz) green salad mix or shredded lettuce

60 ml (2 fl oz) sweet chili sauce

2 large tomatoes, sliced

250 ml (8 fl oz) traditional tartare sauce

30 g (1 oz) finely chopped spring onions

dill sprigs, to garnish

METHOD

- Place the fish fillets on a plate. Sprinkle both sides with seasoning. Cut the pide bread in half. Spread lightly with the butter. Prepare the filling ingredients. Take all to the barbecue area.
- Prepare the barbecue for direct-heat cooking. Heat to medium-high heat. Grease the grill bars well. Brush the fish with oil, place on the grill bars and cook for 3 minutes each side or until cooked through.
- Place the pide on the barbecue, crust side down, to heat a little, turn butter side down to lightly toast.
- To assemble, place the lettuce on the base of each portion of pide bread, drizzle very lightly with the chili sauce if desired. Top with 3 tomato slices. Place on the grilled fish, top with tartare sauce and sprinkle with chopped spring onion and a sprig of dill. Place on the top piece of pide.

Mussel Fritters

INGREDIENTS

24 mussels
15 ml (½ fl oz) oil
1 onion, finely chopped
1 clove garlic, chopped
1 stick lemongrass, bruised
  and cut in half lengthwise
1 teaspoon chili paste
15 g (½ oz) mild curry powder
125 ml (4 fl oz) coconut milk
2 eggs
125 g (4 oz) cornflour
1 teaspoon baking powder
lemon wedges, to serve

METHOD

- Debeard, wash and boil the mussles for 3–5 minutes. Shell the mussels and set aside.
- Heat the oil in a medium-sized saucepan. Sauté the onion, garlic and lemongrass for 5 minutes or until the onion turns clear. Add the chili and curry powder and cook over a low heat for 1 to 2 minutes or until spices smell fragrant. Remove from heat, remove the lemongrass stick and add the coconut milk and eggs. Beat with a fork until combined.
- Place mussels in a food processor and add mixture from saucepan, cornflour and baking powder and process until the mussels are roughly chopped and the mixture is combined. If you don't have a processor, chop mussels finely and mix all ingredients together until combined.
- Divide the mussel mixture into 8 dollops and place on a hot oiled barbecue hotplate to cook. Turn and cook the second side until golden. Serve hot with fresh lemon wedges.

Salmon Fillets with Thai Sauce

SERVES 4

INGREDIENTS

4 skinless salmon fillets
350 g (12 oz) jasmine rice
125 g (4 oz) sesame seeds
30 ml (1 fl oz) olive oil
250 ml (8 fl oz) Thai marinade
bunch of spring onions (scallions)

Thai Marinade

1 teaspoon sesame oil
1 teaspoon chili oil
1 teaspoon peanut oil
1 onion, grated
2 teaspoons freshly minced garlic
2 teaspoons freshly minced
   ginger
2 red capsicums, roasted,
   deseeded, skin removed and
   finely diced
1 whole lime, juiced
2 teaspoons light soy sauce
15 g (½ oz) freshly ground black
   pepper
60 g (2 oz) brown sugar
1 red chili, cut lengthwise
375 ml (12 fl oz) water
1 teaspoon cornflour (cornstarch)
1 small bunch coriander (cilantro)
   leaves, stalks removed and
   finely chopped

METHOD

- Steam the rice, mix through the sesame seeds and place in a container suitable for reheating.
- Rub the salmon with oil and pour over the Thai marinade, making sure it covers both sides of the fish. Cover and set aside for 20 minutes.
- Cut the spring onions diagonally into 25 mm (1 in) lengths, including some of the green tops. Place onto 2 foil squares, pour over a little of the marinade and wrap into a parcel with a double fold top and sides. Take everything to the barbecue area.
- Prepare the barbecue for direct-heat grilling and heat to hot. Place the steamed rice at edge of the grill to keep hot.
- Oil the grill well. Place the salmon and the foil parcel of spring onions on the grill and cook for 2 minutes. Turn the salmon and the foil parcel and cook for 2 minutes more. Remove the parcel. Cook the salmon until done. Divide the onions between 4 plates on top of a mound of rice and the salmon. Serve immediately.
- To make marinade pour all the oils into a saucepan. Add the onion and fry for 2 minutes, stirring occasionally. Add garlic and ginger and continue to fry for 2 more minutes.
- Add all the other ingredients except the water, cornflour and coriander. Stir the ingredients thoroughly.
- Add a little of the water to the cornflour and work into a paste. Add the rest of the water to the cornflour, and then add the mixture to the pot. Stir to combine and simmer for 10 minutes. Add coriander and cook for another 2 minutes.
- Allow to cool. Remove the 2 chili pieces and transfer marinade to an airtight container. Makes approximately 625 ml (1¼ pints) in finished volume. Can be stored in the refrigerator for approximately 6–8 weeks.

Shrimp and Scallop Skewers

SERVES 6

INGREDIENTS

1 kg (2.2 lb) medium-size
  green jumbo prawns
  (shrimp)

12 scallops

1 red onion, cut in wedges

1 red and 1 yellow capsicum
  (bell pepper), cut into strips

30 ml (1 fl oz) melted butter

90 ml (3 fl oz) sweet chili
  sauce

500 g (1.1 lb) white rice and
  wild rice mix

12 metal or soaked bamboo
  skewers

fresh coriander (cilantro)
  leaves, for garnish

METHOD

- Remove the prawn heads but leave the tails on. Peel and devein the prawns. Thread 2–3 prawns, 1 wedge of onion, yellow capsicum and red capsicum, and 2 scallops alternately onto each skewer. Brush with melted butter.
- Prepare the rice according to packet instructions. Place in a heatproof dish suitable for reheating on the barbecue.
- Prepare the barbecue for direct-heat cooking, heat to hot and oil the grill bars well. Place the bowl of rice at the side of the grill to heat. Place the skewers on the grill and cook for 2–3 minutes each side, brushing with chili sauce as they cook. If charring occurs place a sheet of baking paper onto the grill, transfer the skewers on top and continue to cook until done.
- Spread the wild rice mixture on a platter and set the skewers on top. Garnish with coriander leaves. Serve immediately.

Moroccan Fish
with Fresh Tomato Sauce

SERVES 4

INGREDIENTS

750 g (1 lb 8 oz) white fish
  fillets, skinned
1 medium red onion, finely
  chopped
1 clove garlic, crushed
60 g (2 oz) fresh coriander
  (cilantro), chopped
90 g (3 oz) up fresh flat-leaf
  parsley, chopped
½ teaspoon ground sweet
  paprika
¼ teaspoon chili powder
90 ml (3 fl oz) olive oil
30 ml (1 fl oz) lemon juice

Tomato Sauce
4 large tomatoes, peeled,
  deseeded and chopped
2 small red chilies, deseeded
  and finely sliced
4 spring onions (scallions),
  finely sliced
½ bunch fresh coriander
  (cilantro), finely chopped
125 ml (4 fl oz) olive oil
freshly ground black pepper
1 teaspoon lime juice
1 red onion, finely chopped

METHOD

- Cut fish across grain into 2 cm (¾ in) cubes. Combine onion, garlic, coriander, parsley, paprika, chili powder, olive oil and lemon juice and spoon over fish. Mix well and leave to marinate for at least 2 hours or overnight.
- Place fish on metal skewers and grill, turning frequently, until lightly browned on all sides.
- To make tomato sauce, combine tomatoes, chilies, spring onions and coriander in a bowl, then add olive oil and pepper to taste. Add lime juice and red onion. Refrigerate the tomato sauce for at least 1 hour before serving with fish.

Pizzas

Pizza alle Vongole

MAKES 1 PIZZA

INGREDIENTS

250 g (8 oz) peeled, deseeded and chopped tomatoes

60 ml (2 fl oz) olive oil

4 sprigs fresh oregano, leaves removed and finely chopped

1 quantity Neapolitan pizza dough (see page 205)

15 g (½ oz) chopped garlic

125 ml (4 fl oz) dry white wine

750 g (1 lb 8 oz) small clams or mussels

60 g (2 oz) flat-leaf parsley, coarsely chopped

METHOD

- Preheat oven to 240°C (475°F).
- In a small bowl, combine tomatoes, 30 ml (1 fl oz) of the olive oil and the oregano, let stand 15 minutes.
- Shape pizza dough and brush dough with 30 ml (1 fl oz) of the liquid from the tomatoes. Spoon tomatoes over dough. Bake until well-browned and puffy (about 18 minutes). Remove from oven and set aside.
- While pizza is baking, heat remaining oil over moderately low heat in frying pan large enough to hold all the clams. Add garlic and sauté until fragrant but not browned (about 2 minutes). Add wine, raise heat to high and bring to the boil.
- Add clams, cover and steam until they open (about 3–5 minutes), shaking occasionally and removing any clams that have opened. Discard any clams that haven't opened after 5 minutes.
- Remove clam meat from shells and discard shells. Return clams to frying pan. Add parsley and remove from heat. Scatter clams over the baked pizza and serve hot.

Pizza Côte d'Azur

MAKES 1 PIZZA

INGREDIENTS

60 ml (2 fl oz) olive oil

2 onions, thinly slivered

2 cloves garlic, chopped

½ teaspoon dried herbes de Provence

60 g (2 oz) flat-leaf parsley, coarsely chopped

1 quantity Neapolitan pizza dough (see page 205)

1 quantity Basic Tomato Sauce (see page 201)

125 g (4 oz) Gruyère cheese, grated

60 g (2 oz) anchovy fillets, well drained

60 g (2 oz) small niçoise olives

METHOD

- Preheat oven to 230°C (450°F).
- Heat oil in a large frying pan over moderate heat. Add onions and cook, stirring often, until soft but not browned (10–12 minutes), then remove from heat.
- Spoon about 15 ml (½ fl oz) of the hot oil from the pan into a small bowl, then mix in garlic, herbes de Provence and parsley.
- Shape pizza dough and spread sauce over the pizza, sprinkle evenly with cheese. Spread onions over cheese. Arrange anchovies and olives over onions. Sprinkle evenly with garlic-and-herb mixture.
- Bake until crust is well-browned (20–25 minutes). Serve hot.
- This pizza is flavoured with herbes de Provence, a commercial blend of dried thyme, lavender, summer savoury, basil and rosemary – herbs typical of the south of France.

Salmon and Avocado Pizza

MAKES 1 PIZZA

INGREDIENTS

1 quantity Basic Pizza Dough
  (see page 204)
200 g (7 oz) ricotta cheese,
  drained
30 g (1 oz) fresh dill, chopped
1 tablespoon fresh lemon
  thyme, chopped
250 g (8 oz) smoked salmon,
  sliced
1 avocado, sliced
15 g (½ oz) capers, drained
125 g (4 oz) cherry tomatoes,
  halved

METHOD

- Preheat oven to 200°C (400°F).
- Prepare pizza dough, then press dough into a buttered 26 x 32 cm (9 x 13 in) Swiss roll tin. Set aside.
- Place ricotta cheese, dill and thyme in a bowl and mix to combine. Spread ricotta mixture over pizza base and bake for 15 minutes.
- Top pizza with smoked salmon, avocado slices, capers and tomatoes. Reduce oven temperature to 180°C (360°F) and bake for 10 minutes longer or until heated through and base is crisp and golden.

Smoked Salmon Pizzas

MAKES 4 SMALL PIZZAS

INGREDIENTS

1 quantity Basic Pizza Dough
(see page 204)

15 ml (½ oz) olive oil

200 g (7 oz) smoked salmon
slices

freshly ground black pepper

60 ml (2 fl oz) crème fraîche
or sour cream

4 teaspoons salmon caviar

60 g (2 oz) fresh lemon
thyme, chopped

METHOD

- Preheat oven to 200°C (400°F).
- Prepare pizza dough. Divide into four portions and shape each to form a 15 cm (6 in) round. Place rounds on lightly buttered baking trays, brush with oil and bake for 15 minutes or until crisp and golden.
- Reduce oven temperature to 180°C (360°F). Top pizzas with smoked salmon and black pepper to taste and bake for 8 minutes or until salmon is hot.
- Just prior to serving, top pizzas with crème fraîche and caviar and sprinkle with thyme.

Pizza with Monkfish

INGREDIENTS

250 g (8 oz) plain flour
salt and freshly ground black
  pepper
15 g (½ oz) fresh yeast
½ teaspoon sunflower oil
400 g (14 oz) skinless,
  boneless monkfish or other
  firm white fish fillets
60 ml (2 fl oz) olive oil
4 French shallots, finely
  chopped
200 g (7 oz) tomatoes, cut
  into chunks
1 clove garlic, thinly sliced
5 fresh basil leaves
400 g (14 oz) mozzarella
  cheese, sliced
fresh basil sprigs, to garnish

METHOD

- Sift the flour into a bowl and add a large pinch of salt. Make a well in the centre of the flour and crumble in the yeast. Add about 125 ml (4 fl oz) lukewarm water and the sunflower oil and stir to dissolve the yeast.
- Set aside for 10 minutes before kneading the mixture to a smooth dough. Cover the bowl and set aside in a warm place for about 1 hour, until risen and doubled in size.
- Cut the fish into cubes and set aside.
- Heat the olive oil in a pan and cook the shallots until softened. Add the fish and tomatoes and season to taste with salt and pepper. Add the garlic and basil and stir to mix. Cook gently for 5 minutes, stirring occasionally.
- Preheat oven to 220°C (430°F). Roll out the dough on a lightly floured work surface into a large circle and place on a buttered baking tray. Drizzle the pizza base with a little olive oil and spread the fish mixture on top.
- Bake for about 20 minutes, until risen and cooked. Serve hot, garnished with fresh basil sprigs.

Pizza with Mussels

MAKES 2 PIZZAS

INGREDIENTS

300 g (10 oz) plain flour
1 sachet dried yeast
60 ml (2 fl oz) olive oil
1 teaspoon salt
125 ml (4 fl oz) lukewarm milk

Topping

4 tomatoes, skinned
250 g (8 oz) mozzarella
  cheese
10 stuffed Spanish olives
5 small fresh chilies
500 g (16 oz) cooked, shelled
  mussels
½ teaspoon dried oregano
½ teaspoon dried basil
½ teaspoon dried rosemary
60 ml (2 fl oz) olive oil

METHOD

- Preheat oven to at 220°C (430°F).
- Sift the flour into a bowl and mix in the dried yeast thoroughly before adding the olive oil, salt and lukewarm milk to form a dough. Knead the dough for about 5 minutes. If the dough is too sticky, sprinkle over a little extra flour but take care not to add too much so that the dough remains workable. Set aside the dough in a warm place until risen and doubled in size.
- Knead the dough again and divide in half. Roll out each half of dough to make 2 pizza bases about 20 cm (8 in) in diameter. Place on a buttered baking sheet.
- For the topping, dice the tomatoes and cheese and slice the stuffed olives. Finely chop the chilies. Divide the mussels, tomatoes, cheese, olives and chilies evenly between the 2 pizza bases.
- Sprinkle oregano, basil and rosemary over the topping, then drizzle over the olive oil.
- Bake for about 25 minutes, until golden and bubbling. Serve hot.

Seafood Pizza

MAKES 1 PIZZA

INGREDIENTS

250 g (8 oz) fresh cockles
500 g (16 oz) fresh
   mussels
125 ml (4 fl oz) white wine
1 quantity Basic Pizza
   Dough (see page 204)
1 quantity Basic Tomato
   Sauce
1 large onion, thinly sliced
2 cloves garlic, chopped
1 teaspoon dried marjoram
salt and freshly ground
   black pepper
30 g (1 oz) Parmesan
   cheese, grated

Basic Tomato Sauce

60 g (2 oz) fresh basil,
   chopped
½ teaspoon dried oregano
30 ml (1 fl oz) white wine
¼ medium onion, grated
1 clove garlic, chopped
1 teaspoon olive oil
2 tomatoes peeled,
   deseeded and chopped
1½ teaspoons tomato
   paste

METHOD

- Wash, brush and rinse the cockles and mussels thoroughly. Place them in a large saucepan, pour over the wine and place over a high heat, shaking the pan frequently until all the shells have opened. Set the pan aside to allow the contents to cool.
- Once the cockles and mussels are cooled, remove from their shells, discarding any that have not opened. Discard the juices.
- Preheat oven to 220°C (430°F). Roll out the pizza dough into a large round on a lightly floured work surface. Place on a baking tray.
- Pour the tomato sauce into the centre of the pizza and spread over the dough with the back of a spoon.
- Place the sliced onion over the tomato sauce, then place the mussels and cockles on top.
- Scatter over the garlic, season with marjoram and salt and pepper and top with Parmesan cheese.
- Bake for about 15–25 minutes, depending on the thickness of the dough. Serve immediately.
- To make tomato sauce: In a small bowl, steep basil and oregano in white wine for 10 minutes.
- In a frying pan over medium-high heat, sauté onion and garlic in olive oil for 5 minutes, stirring frequently. Add tomatoes and tomato paste, then steeped herbs and wine. Cover, reduce heat and simmer 15 minutes.
- Remove sauce from heat and purée in a blender or food processor.
- The secret to the flavour of this quick, low-fat sauce, which uses very little oil, is steeping the basil and oregano in wine before cooking. This simple step draws out the flavour of the herbs, creating a sauce that tastes as if it had been cooking for hours. This recipe calls for fresh tomatoes, but you may also use canned tomatoes.

Mini Prawn Pizzas

INGREDIENTS

1 teaspoon fresh yeast

250 g (8 oz) plain flour

½ teaspoon salt

½ teaspoon sugar

30 ml (1 fl oz) olive oil

300 g (10 oz) cooked, shelled
  prawns (shrimp)

1 egg

15 ml (½ fl oz) crème fraîche

salt and freshly ground black
  pepper

lemon pepper

60 g (2 oz) fresh parsley

150 g (5 oz) fresh Parmesan
  cheese, grated

METHOD

- Preheat oven to 220°C (430°F).
- In a bowl, carefully mix the yeast with the flour, then add the salt, sugar, olive oil and 125 ml (4 fl oz) lukewarm water. Mix thoroughly to form a smooth dough.
- Knead the dough for about 5 minutes, then cover and set aside in a warm place until risen and doubled in size.
- Divide the dough into 6 equal portions and roll out each one into a round. Place on buttered baking trays.
- Spread the prawns evenly over the pizza bases and set aside. In a bowl, beat the egg into the crème fraîche, stir in the seasoning and cover the prawns evenly with the sauce. Sprinkle the pizzas with chopped parsley and grated Parmesan cheese.
- Bake for 20 minutes, until risen and cooked. Serve hot.

Basic Pizza Dough

MAKES 1 PIZZA CRUST

INGREDIENTS

1½ teaspoons dry yeast
pinch sugar
375 ml (12 fl oz) warm water,
   about 41°C (105°F)
125 ml (4 fl oz) olive oil
500 g (8 oz) plain flour, sifted
1¼ teaspoons salt
olive oil, for bowl, as needed

METHOD

- In a small bowl dissolve yeast and sugar in the warm water and let stand 5 minutes. Stir in olive oil. In a large bowl combine flour and salt. Add yeast mixture and stir until dough just barely holds together.
- Turn dough out on a lightly floured surface and knead until smooth and silky, adding a little more flour if dough seems sticky. Put dough in an oiled bowl and turn to coat surface with oil. Cover bowl with cling wrap and let rise in a warm place until doubled in bulk (about 1 hour).
- After dough has risen until doubled in bulk, punch it down, using your fist in a straight-down motion.
- To shape into pizza crust, on lightly floured surface, roll dough out to desired size. Place on baker's peel or oiled pizza pan dusted with cornmeal. Any excess dough can be wrapped in plastic kitchen wrap and kept in the refrigerator.

- Note: A simple, straightforward dough enriched with oil, this one is ready to use in a little more than an hour. For a firm, elastic dough that yields a crisp, finely textured crust, replace up to half the flour with semolina, a high-protein flour ground from hard durum wheat.

Neapolitan Pizza Dough

MAKES 1 PIZZA CRUST

INGREDIENTS

7 g (¼ oz) dry yeast
300ml (10 fl oz) warm water,
  about 41°C (105°F)
300 g (10½ oz) plain flour
½ teaspoon salt

METHOD

- In a medium bowl dissolve yeast in the water. Add 150 g (10 oz) of the flour and mix well to make a sponge or soft batter-like dough. Cover with cling wrap and let rise 45 minutes.
- In a large bowl, combine remaining flour and the salt. Add risen dough and mix well. Turn out onto a lightly floured surface and knead until smooth and silky (about 5 minutes), adding flour as necessary. Put dough in an oiled bowl and turn to coat evenly. Cover and let rise 2 hours.
- Punch the dough down punch using your fist in a straight-down motion.
- To shape into pizza crust, on lightly floured surface, roll dough out to desired size. Place on baker's peel or oiled pizza pan dusted with cornmeal. Any excess dough can be wrapped in plastic kitchen wrap and kept in the refrigerator.

- Note: This classic Neapolitan pizza dough yields a dry crisp crust that can support a moist topping, such as fresh clams. The recipe contains no oil other than what is used for oiling the bowl and the dough prior to rising. Allowing the dough to rise twice produces a pleasing, yeasty flavour.

INDEX

First published in 2017 by New Holland Publishers Pty Ltd
London • Sydney • Auckland

The Chandlery Unit 704 50 Westminster Bridge Road London SE1 7QY United Kingdom
1/66 Gibbes Street Chatswood NSW 2067 Australia
5/39 Woodside Ave Northcote, Auckland 0627 New Zealand

www.newhollandpublishers.com

A record of this book is held at the British Library and the National Library of Australia.

ISBN: 9781742579238

Group Managing Director: Fiona Schultz
Editor: Bill Twyman
Designer: Lorena Susak
Production Director: James Mills-Hicks

Printer: Toppan Leefung Printing Limited

10 9 8 7 6 5 4 3 2 1

Keep up with New Holland Publishers on Facebook
www.facebook.com/NewHollandPublishers